Church Growth

Creative Leadership Series

Assimilating New Members, Lyle E. Schaller
Beginning a New Pastorate, Robert G. Kemper
The Care and Feeding of Volunteers, Douglas W. Johnson
Creative Stewardship, Richard B. Cunningham
Time Management, Speed B. Leas
Your Church Can Be Healthy, C. Peter Wagner
Leading Churches Through Change, Douglas Alan Walrath
Building an Effective Youth Ministry, Glenn E. Ludwig
Preaching and Worship in the Small Church,
William Willimon and Robert L. Wilson

Church Growth
Strategies That Work

Donald McGavran & George G. Hunter III

Creative Leadership Series
Lyle E. Schaller, Editor

Abingdon / Nashville

CHURCH GROWTH: STRATEGIES THAT WORK

Copyright © 1980 by Abingdon

Library of Congress Cataloging in Publication Data

MCGAVRAN, DONALD ANDERSON, 1897-
   Church growth.
   (Creative leadership series)
   1. Church growth. I. Hunter, George G., joint author. II. Title.
   III. Series.
   BV652.25.M26   254'.5   79-26962

IBSN 0-687-08160-2

MANUFACTURED BY THE PARTHENON PRESS AT
NASHVILLE, TENNESSEE, UNITED STATES OF AMERICA

To our two beloved
secretaries and colleagues,
Josephine Hicks and Frances Junker
with deep and abiding appreciation

Foreword

From this observer's perspective the most significant development on the American religious scene during the past half century was the emergence of the Charismatic Renewal Movement during the 1960s. In a more recent and shorter time frame the most influential development of the 1970s was the emergence of the church growth movement. The "father" of that movement is Dr. Donald McGavran, the coauthor of this volume in the Creative Leadership Series.

In this book Dr. McGavran and Dr. George G. Hunter have produced an excellent introduction to the church growth movement. They also have distilled from the twenty years of research on church growth the basic lessons that constitute the foundation for a congregational strategy for church growth.

In studying this volume there are four points that the

reader may want to keep in mind when considering how these basic concepts apply "back home in our church." First, in very pragmatic terms, the basic principles do work! Hundreds of congregations that have been on a plateau or reporting numerical decline year after year have applied basic church growth principles and found they do work. The numerically declining church can be turned around and can become a growing church.

Second, while the pastor is a very important factor in church growth, the critical variable is in the attitudes of the members. If the members are unwilling to implement those operational decisions necessary to encourage church growth, it is unlikely the congregation will grow except in those rare situations where the population growth in the community is such as to cause all congregations to grow.

Third, most congregations already have more members than they can care for; therefore it is essential that a church growth strategy also include an operational plan for the assimilation of new members.

Fourth, numerical growth usually brings unanticipated changes with it. Some of these changes may cause a few of the "old pillars" of the congregation to feel alienated from what to them is a "new" congregation. Therefore the growth strategy should include provision for the careful continuing care of the long-time members who might feel alienated by the pace of change.

These comments should not be viewed as warnings against church growth, but simply as precautionary observations that may help creative leaders produce a more comprehensive plan for church growth.

As with the earlier volumes in this series, this book is designed to be used as a source of guidance by ministers and congregational leaders as they seek to discover and implement God's will for that particular congregation. As they study what Dr. McGavran and Dr. Hunter have to offer, they will discover exciting new possibilities for church growth.

Lyle E. Schaller
Yokefellow Institute
Richmond, Indiana

Contents

I

The Discovery of
Church Growth

The Scene Today

We stand today in the midst of a truly extraordinary interest in church growth. Everyone is talking about it. Church growth seminars are held from Alaska to Miami. Books on church growth pour from the presses. Articles on church growth appear in many magazines. Church growth courses are given in seminaries and colleges.

The interest is all the more remarkable when it is observed that ten or fifteen years ago the words were never seen. On the contrary, the growth of the church was often castigated as an unworthy aim, as capitalistic, imperialistic, or triumphalistic. That negativism is not substantially reversed. Many churches and denominations—including a growing number of mainline Protestant denominations from Episcopal to Methodist to Southern Baptist—are eagerly engaging in church growth researches and in regional and national church growth programs.

Please do not think that everyone is for church growth. Opposition to it also marks our time. Since 1960 a new theory and theology of mission has seized leaders of many denominations. They are convinced that today what the churches ought to be doing is *not* evangelism and church growth. Instead, they ought to be rooting out racism, stopping sexism, increasing brotherhood, smashing oppressive social structures, and destroying everything that diminishes human dignity. Only these goals, they maintain, suit Christians in the contemporary world. However, the deliberate turning away from evangelism and church growth is one of the chief reasons for the stagnant condition of so many congregations and denominations today.

We shall explore this tension, in which good people are arrayed on both sides. The issues are tremendous. The days are short. Every move must be made in a way that will count. There is, in short, great urgency in understanding church growth and seeing what it can and cannot do in the current scene.

That is why we shall first look at how the church growth movement arose. This will help us understand its essential characteristics and discover the best way to use it to fulfill God's commission for his American churches.

How We Discovered Church Growth

Many people have been involved in the discovery of church growth. While God has granted me a part in the process, I neither invented church growth nor am solely responsible for it. Indeed, I owe my interest in church growth to a great Methodist bishop, Jarrell Waskom Pickett. In 1934, he kindled my concern that the Church grow. I lit my candle at his fire. The Wesleyan Movement, which has been responsible for explosive church growth around the world for the last two centuries, was promoting church growth long before I was born. And the Church has grown in many periods and cultures. Church growth has always been characteristic of *healthy* churches and basic to the power of the Christian movement. Today's church growth movement has, however, *re*discovered church growth.

But a strange thing has happened in this century. The

missionary movement, which at the outset was focused exclusively on carrying out the Great Commission, and based solidly on the ancient conviction that the Gospel was for all people, regardless of race, religion, tribe, or nationality, became excessively concerned with other things than communicating that Gospel to the peoples of the earth. World mission began to hold that its main task was helping younger churches and training their leaders. It observed that where the Christian mission went, it influenced social structures and changed some of them in the direction of justice and mercy. So the assumption evolved that social action and the changing of social structures were *basic* functions of the Christian mission. Even evangelism became more and more "renewal," an effort to make existing Christians better Christians. Church growth from among the hundreds of millions of *non*-Christians was downgraded, eclipsed, ignored.

Some ministers, missionaries, and other Christians were not aware of these trends; but to me in India, they became plain. In the early 1930s, I found increasingly the need to focus on the growth of the Church, the conversion of millions who have yet to believe, and the formation of hundreds of thousands of new congregations. These new units of peace and justice, where life revolves around Jesus Christ and his Word, are essential to the formation of that just world all Christians deeply want.

In the mid-thirties I was the executive secretary-treasurer of the India Mission of the Disciples of Christ—one of the larger missions in India, with more than eighty missionaries at work in 1930. All the money and the accounts passed through my hands. I preached in the churches, knew intimately the pastors and missionaries, and observed that this massive outlay of men and money did not result in commensurate church growth. Of our seventeen congregations not one was growing. I wondered why. We had only two thousand communicant members after more than fifty years of work.

15

Furthermore our stalled situation was duplicated in 136 out of 165 mission stations in the whole of Mid-India. Methodists, Presbyterians, Lutherans, Quakers, and Episcopalians were as stalled as we were.

I knew perfectly well that church growth is dependent on the action of the Holy Spirit, but since God works in orderly ways and, according to Scripture, does not want *any* to perish, I believed that the Holy Spirit wanted more growth than we were getting. I came to believe that nongrowth is a disease, but a *curable* disease. I came increasingly to believe that God wanted more growth than we were getting and that if we would but go about Christian mission in an enlightened way, God would grant us more church growth.

Among our church leaders and missionaries, recognition of the disease of slow growth was blocked by certain rationalizations of defeat that had become common among us. Of these, one was that we were evangelizing *in India* and "everyone knew" that in India very few Hindus and Muslims became Christians. Another was that our national and American leaders did not pray enough, had too many disagreements, and, in a word, were not sanctified enough.

Neither rationalization impressed me. For, as Pickett pointed out, in other parts of India the church had grown greatly; and I observed that where the church grew, the leaders were not more sanctified than we were. A vast curiosity was born within me. What *does* make churches grow? More importantly, what makes many churches *stop* growing? How is it possible for Christians to come out of ripe harvest fields empty-handed? Answering the questions, What are the *causes* of church growth? and What are the *obstacles* to church growth? became the chief purpose of my life.

From 1937 to 1954—seventeen long years—I worked as a frontline missionary in the heart of India. I did everything that most missionaries do—educational work, leprosy relief, hospital work, famine relief, rural reconstruction, and evangelism. I did all these with one single aim—that through them men and women might come to know Jesus Christ as Lord and Savior and become responsible members of his Body, the Church.

I was neither writing books nor lecturing in those days. I was working, and often coming empty-handed out of ripe fields and wondering why. I wish I could report huge° success, but that is not what I saw. After seventeen years, perhaps a thousand Christians were there as a result of my labors. They had been gathered into the existing churches and into perhaps a dozen new churches out in the villages. That was all.

Other missions during those years sometimes called me to survey their fields from the church growth point of view. I studied Mennonite, Methodist, Presbyterian, and Anglican fields, observing what procedures God was blessing to the growth of his churches and what he was not. Thus I formed and tested many principles of church growth. During those long, hard years God granted me considerable insight into how churches grow. The basic theory and theology of the church growth movement was being hammered out on the anvil of the disciplined observance and analysis of the Church's experience among many peoples of India. In 1954 I visited seven nations in Africa, studied the churches established there by twenty missionary societies, and tested my insights concerning church growth against the very different African conditions.

All these insights I gathered together and published in *Bridges of God*,[1] which, in 1955 and 1956, created a phenomenal interest all around the world. The interest proved short-lived. The static view of missions, the shift of the focus from the growth of the Church to good deeds done by Western churches and to interchurch aid had been too complete for one book to change the trend. I then wrote *How Churches Grow*,[2] which was published in England by World Dominion Press and in America by Friendship Press. This, too, was widely read. But like *Bridges of God*, it produced no noticeable shift in missionary policy, allocation of funds or sendings of missionaries.

Between 1956 and 1960, the United Christian Missionary Society sent me to Latin America, the Philippines, Thailand, and the Caribbean to survey the churches it had founded in each of those lands. I had to adjust church growth theory to make it valid in each new population and for all populations. The Indian color was replaced by a global way of thinking. During the years 1960 to 1970, we systematized the concepts and principles of the church growth movement and fitted them to five continents, to all, in fact, except North America. My findings were published in *Understanding Church Growth*,[3] which many regard as the foundation of the church growth movement.

Since the early 1960s, I have had a growing number of colleagues in this general enterprise. I began in 1961, at Northwest Christian College, an Institute for Church Growth. This was moved to Pasadena, California, in 1965 as I became the Founding Dean of Fuller Theological Seminary School of World Mission. There my colleagues, notably Alan Tippett, C. Peter Wagner, Arthur Glasser, and Ralph Winter have expanded church growth thinking—as have our numerous career missionaries from many lands and tongues. We are confident we have proven that responsible research sheds much light on how churches grow and stop growing, and that the social sciences can be harnessed to further the spread of the Gospel and the growth of the Church.

It soon became apparent that throughout the world a major block in refocusing attention on the millions who have yet to believe, on effective evangelism among non-Christians, and on the objective growth of the Church was the substantial wall of rationalizations that ministers and missionaries had built up *against* church growth. Since they had been getting but slight growth, they had explained *non*growth to themselves as inevitable, as natural, as,

18

indeed, God's will, clearly foretold in the Bible. When the light of truth fell on these rationalizations, they turned out to be nothing more than excuses, having no biblical base. As the Institute of Church Growth explained them, and gently laughed at them, these excuses gradually were abandoned. When church growth is attacked today, it is usually done by persons who, not having had the opportunity to think their way through the morass, are comforting themselves with the old rationalizations of defeat.

When a minister first uses the term "church growth," he is likely to think that it concerns merely getting more members in his church. Under the pressure of old rationalizations of nongrowth, he equates it with "numerolatry," the tyranny of statistics, and other similar cop outs. In radical opposition to this idea, it soon became apparent to me that church growth had very large dimensions. It was no mere gimmick to get more people and money into the church. *Its foundation was theological.* It was based on a biblical judgment that men and women without Jesus Christ are truly lost and God wants them found. So, church growth is faithfulness to God. When God sends harvesters into ripe fields, he wants them to come out bearing sheaves. God wants his lost children found, and there are millions of them.

How America Is Discovering Church Growth

America is discovering church growth. Mainline denominations are waking to its urgency. This is timely, as we see afresh that the United States is a mission field with millions of undiscipled people. We ignored God's purpose for a time, but he will not be forever denied. He stands at the door and knocks. He steadily demands that the Gospel be shared effectively. He meets ministers, as he met John Wesley, and they become apostles. He invades the hearts of lay people, as he did that of John R. Mott, and they spend entire lifetimes proclaiming Christ and multiplying churches.

19

In the seventies the time for American church growth had come. By 1960 the slight spurt after World War II had ended. *Many* denominations plateaued with church membership stuck at six thousand, two hundred thousand, and ten million. Some congregations gained a little. Others lost a little and the denomination's graph of membership continued on a dead level. A number of denominations actually declined, losing a few thousand or a few hundred thousand members. Worse, these denominations were *content* to be plateaued or declining. They were too respectable, too spiritual (so they said) to want to grow. Their leaders congratulated themselves on resisting the tyranny of statistics. Strident voices demanded quality, not quantity, and purging, not growth. No wonder plateaus and declines continued.

Research by Professor Russell Hale, of Gettysburg Theological Seminary, concludes that eighty million men and women consciously remain out of the Church. "Masses of Americans have nothing whatsoever to do with the Church." To these eighty million, add seventy million more who are baptized and have their names on church rolls somewhere, attend occasionally, but are mere nominal members who live according to their own desires and are the centers of their tiny worlds. A hundred and fifty million lost people in America! And many of them are receptive and searching. What a tremendous opportunity for church growth. American church growth is an idea whose time has come.

The American Beginning

In September, 1971, Dr. C. Peter Wagner determined to expose twenty-five leading ministers and laypersons of the Pasadena area to church growth thinking. He set up a class that met in the Lake Avenue Congregational Church in Pasadena on Tuesday mornings for three hours. Regular seminary credit was offered and tuition charged. A heavy reading schedule was involved. Wagner asked me to team-teach the course with him. We had a very good time. The ministers brought up all the old, tired excuses and objections. We examined them carefully and tenderly laid them to rest. Once these pastors got over their hang-ups, they consumed church growth. It spoke to their real needs. It opened the way across America for a series of similar classes in the months ahead. Dr. Wagner devised church growth courses on the level of the doctor of ministries, and by now some hundreds of work-a-day ministers have taken them. Wagner has since published *Your Church Can Grow*,[4] and *Your Church Can Be Healthy*.[5] He launched an American Church Growth Book Club.

One of our students at Lake Avenue was Dr. Winfield Arn, who was then Secretary for Christian Education for the Evangelical Covenant Church in the six southwestern states. His eyes gleamed. He saw visions and dreamed dreams. He resigned his job as denominational executive and started the Institute for American Church Growth. He made four sound color pictures presenting the church growth message: *How to Grow a Church, Reach Out and Grow, They Said It Couldn't Be Done*, and *Planned Parenthood for Churches*. These have been seen in thousands of American churches. He devised church growth seminars. He and his staff have been called all across America from the Carolinas to Alaska. Last year more than sixteen thousand ministers and lay leaders attended these seminars. Dr. Arn began publishing the magazine *Church Growth: America*. It now has a circulation of over twenty-five thousand. With me he jointly authored *How to Grow a Church*[6] and *Ten Steps to Church Growth*.[7]

The church growth movement found tinder lying ready to hand across North America. Pastors were tired of static churches and welcomed light on growth. They wanted to see new churches planted and old churches reaching out

21

with power. The heart of the Church still believed that it was commanded to make disciples of all peoples at home and abroad. Individual congregations came alive. Whole denominations began to pray and plan for effective evangelism. Books by the dozen were published. The Reformed Church of America, the Southern Baptists, Annual Meetings of the Society of Friends, Free Methodists, Episcopalians, and United Methodists, all became deeply involved in church growth.

Many churches that geared for growth have experienced growth. Since 1965, the Southern Baptist thrust in the seven central northern states has lifted total membership from two hundred thousand to four hundred thousand. Churches in the United States in varying degrees are becoming aware of their calling and opportunities in a new way. We are increasingly perceiving that all men and women have the inalienable right to follow Jesus Christ and be members of his special family, a basic human right too often denied or ignored in the recent past.

Today all across North America, in Canada as well as the United States, church leaders with major responsibilities are gathering to study the theory and practice of church growth. One denomination reports that forty-five district superintendents "had four of the most productive, stimulating days we have ever had immersed in church growth." Another mainline denomination gathered three bishops and 170 clergy to study their growth patterns and in particular the growth patterns of those congregations that, despite the general trend down, were manifesting healthy growth. One denomination, which has been plateaued for twenty years, asked all its pastors where their churches get their prospects for an in-flow of new people. Answers indicated that the strongest stream coming in was composed of new people "brought or recommended by members."

Thousands of eminent church leaders are now operating

on the revolutionary assumption that a *healthy church grows.* Physical growth is not everything, of course. But every father would be deeply troubled if his son at sixteen weighed the same eighty pounds that he did at twelve. Healthy, normal churches grow. They feed on God's Word, worship and obey the Head of the Church, practice their Christian faith, and are deeply concerned about the pagans inhabiting their very neighborhoods. Not only are they concerned, but they do something about it. Not only do they do something, they keep on experimenting, and praying, and changing methods until they find a potent combination of activities that brings a stream of new men and women to Christian faith.

The executive director of a great home missionary society recently set forth the following purposes of his organization:

1. To discover and enunciate a philosophy of church growth which is workable for and by our people
2. To learn the difference between what is church growth and what is not; and to focus attention on how church management, evangelism, discipling and body life do and do not contribute to the actual growth of our congregations
3. To recognize and renounce the attitudes and cliches in our denomination which stigmatize growth and keep our congregations from wanting to grow
4. To develop in our churches the habit of viewing all neighborhoods as potential parishes, and estimating their receptiveness

As we visited, this executive said to me, "Ten years ago the ministerial circles I move in would have scorned each of these four purposes. I could not then have gained denominational support for them. Today, when I announce them, my colleagues are pleased." What a change of climate!

Hundreds of other illustrations can be given of the ways in which North America is rousing to its shepherd responsibility. Seldom now do we find shepherds gathering at the door of the fold to sneer at finding lost sheep. When they start out to look for lost sheep, they no longer announce loudly, "This is a token search. We are going out to beat the bushes. It really makes no difference how many we find. Our real purpose is something else." One of the most cheering signs of the times is a new seriousness about communicating Christ, a new high doctrine of the Church and the necessity for membership in it, a new enthusiasm concerning the salvific task of the Body of Christ.

Let me hastily add that while North America is waking to church growth, it is still quite comfortable in its warm bed. In huge America, many denominations can get growth of a few hundred thousand each, without materially diminishing the 110 million Americans who are very nominal Christians or the 55 million who are intentionally non-Christians. I want to see the mainline denominations set significant church growth goals. I want to see denominations grow at 8 percent a year! Practicing Christians and their leaders must not congratulate themselves too soon.

The battle has been fairly joined, but it is a long way from being won. Various sects proliferate across this land. People serve their nation and defend their culture as though both were divine. Pagan practices flourish. The worship of Venus, Baal, and phallic symbols multiplies.

America is experiencing new floods of ethnic immigrants who have great needs and who are most responsive when approached intelligently. Eighty thousand Muslims from the Near East have recently moved to Detroit and intend to become citizens of the United States. They see the evidences of decadence mentioned, and conclude that Muhammad not Christ is the real savior of mankind. Hispanic-Americans are surging in in record numbers. Koreans are rushing to America. Most of the Christians coming to Los Angeles from Korea are Presbyterians; but it was the Baptists, not the United Presbyterians, who in the last five years started sixty-two new churches among the incoming multitudes. It is still quite possible to come out of ripe fields empty-handed. Some denominations make it a point of honor to do so!

But Is Church Growth Really Different?

As people are introduced to church growth evangelism, many raise questions regarding its distinctiveness. Is church growth the same old stuff in a new bottle? Or even the same old bottle with a new label? I may be the wrong person to respond to *that* question. I have so much of my life invested in this enterprise that I can hardly be objective.

But in 1974, the coauthor of this book, Dr. George G. Hunter, then professor of evangelism at Perkins School of Theology, Southern Methodist University, began reading church growth literature. His initial approach was at least objective, if not somewhat critical. He came to the conviction that church growth represents a historic new departure for informed evangelization. Now an advocate, he suggests a *dozen* distinctives of the church growth approach:

1. In church growth thought, the *objective* of evangelizing is *to "make disciples,"* actual followers of Jesus Christ, biblically rooted, and incorporated into the Body of Christ. The motive for making new disciples is not self-aggrandizement, but faithfulness to God.
2. Church growth takes *statistics* and *graphs* seriously in analyzing the past record and present situation, and in planning for new church growth.
3. Church growth regards *goal setting* as an indispensable part of a congregation's planned approach to outreach.
4. Church growth people know that no one method of evangelism will engage and elicit response from men and women of all cultures and subcultures. The Church must fashion methods that are *indigenous* to target populations and *effective* in them.

25

5. Church growth harnesses the *social sciences*, especially sociology and cultural anthropology, to develop strategy for the missionary task.
6. Church growth leaders emphasize practical *research* to gain the facts needed for developing evangelism theory and planning for effective Christian expansion.
7. Church growth research constantly *tests* inherited evangelistic principles and methods and *discovers* new ones.
8. Church growth people believe that because of God's prevenient grace, great numbers are *receptive*. Church growth research has discovered *indicators* to enable us to perceive those who might welcome the Gospel and become dependable members of Christ's Church.
9. Church growth emphasizes extensive, even "extravagant," new church planting, believing the Christian movement needs 300,000 more churches in the United States.
10. Church growth strategists now have at their disposal a worldwide data base from church growth research, upon which to predicate theory and strategy.
11. Church growth people hold a high doctrine of the Church, believing that the folding of people into Christ's flock is an essential part of their evangelization.
12. Church growth people are confident that the growth of Christ's Church among the peoples of the earth is the will of God, and he is present to empower her outreach and expansion.

Church growth is not a gimmick. It is faithfulness to God. He wants his lost children found and transformed into responsible members of his Body. The populations in the midst of which God has placed us are the most receptive ever to walk the face of the earth. There are more winnable people today than there have ever been. In these days we must not deceive ourselves by oft-repeated rationalizations of defeat. We must not become keepers of the aquarium. We are "fishers of men."

Most important, if North America is to rediscover church growth, we must pass on to our members our awakened theological convictions concerning church growth, our managerial skills devoted to harvesting ripe fields, and our new awareness of the urgency of finding those potent combinations that God blesses to the increase of his followers. Let us *do* theology and transmit our good words and good intentions into millions of responsible disciples setting their shoulders to the wheel and lifting our churches into positions of social power, devout living, fervent praise, and contagious witness.

II

The Key Strategy:
Finding the Bridges of God

When an American mainline congregation is growing, it is usually reaching out to people who are already in the existing social networks of the church's active disciples, and not especially to "strangers," as the popular evangelical myth assumes. When churches recognize this fact, perceive it as a basic axiom of church growth, and base their programmatic outreach upon it, they will experience unprecedented growth.

This truth, to be demonstrated presently, is America's version of a universal principle of church growth first stated by Donald McGavran in the early fifties.

The Discovery Overseas

Donald McGavran, a missionary to India, learned this principle in its Indian form from Jarrell Waskom Pickett in the early thirties. Pickett's *Christian Mass Movements in India*[1] was addressed to a particular situation—that from the depressed classes very considerable accessions to the Christian faith had taken place. These were initially considered a distinctively Indian phenomenon and called "mass movements." Pickett defended them as a good way for Indian churches to grow *in that social setting*. The following illuminating story shows clearly how the faith spreads within an Indian caste.

Around 1870, a Hindu of the Jat caste named Nattu was converted. He proved to be a source of frustration for the missionaries, but did one day bring to the mission station in Sialkot a new convert whom he had trained, a dark lame little man of the (untouchable) Chuhra caste named Ditt. The missionaries examined Ditt and found him well-instructed and honest in his profession of faith. A problem developed. Established missions policy favored the convert's staying at the mission station for some time for study, the testing of sincerity, and protection from immediate peer persecution—at the end of which the convert was baptized. But Ditt wanted immediate baptism, and he wanted to return to his village, his trade, and his people. The missionary, the Reverend S. Martin, saw that Ditt was determined, so he reluctantly consented and urged Ditt to stick through any persecution and to witness to his neighbors.

The persecution did come. Ditt's five brothers and many relatives refused to eat or associate with him as long as he professed Christianity. But Ditt remained faithful, refused to reject those who rejected him, and as Pickett writes, he triumphed.

> Three months after his baptism he reappeared in Sialkot and presented his wife, his daughter, and two neighbors as candidates for baptism. He had taught them what he knew; they professed their faith and their purpose to follow Christ and had walked thirty miles to be baptized. After examining them, instructing them and praying with them, Mr. Martin administered the rite, whereupon they immediately started back to their village. Six months later Ditt brought four other men who were also adjudged ready for baptism. The missionaries were by now convinced that a work of God was in progress in Ditt's village.[2]

Notice how perceptive the missionaries were! More important, they sensed God leading them toward a more effective missionary strategy. Pickett finishes this splendid account of the effectiveness of a social network in the spread of Christianity as follows:

> Ditt's humble occupation of buying and selling hides took him to many villages. Wherever he went he told his fellow Chuhras of Christ. Many abused him, but an increasing number heard him patiently, and before long groups here and there began to follow his lead. In the eleventh year after Ditt's conversion more than five hundred Chuhras were received into the Church. By 1900, more than half of these lowly people . . . had been converted, and by 1915 all but a few hundred members of the caste professed the Christian faith.[3]

In the early fifties, McGavran's more widespread research discovered that the spread of the Christian faith along existing networks of relationships is not merely an Indian phenomenon confined to the depressed classes of India; it is a universal principle which accounts for much Christian expansion in all ages, countries, and cultures that have known church growth. It applied to Africa, Latin America, Asia, and all mission lands. It was particularly applicable in homogeneous units, that is, in societies that were conscious of themselves as distinct peoples. McGavran tested the principle that Pickett had discerned at work in the depressed classes in India, and his research compelled him to universalize the principle. It may be stated as follows:

The faith spreads most naturally and contagiously along the lines of the social network of living Christians, especially new Christians. Receptive undiscipled men and women usually receive the Possibility when the invitation is extended to them from credible Christian friends, relatives, neighbors, and fellow workers from within their social web.

This universal principle became one of the main elements in McGavran's 1955 bombshell, *The Bridges of God*. Since then it has been abundantly illustrated by studies of church growth in Latin America, Asia, Africa, and other Third World lands.

In the seventies the principle began to be observed in American churches. Once one learns that growth often occurs along the lines of the social network in given units of society, then any Christian can perceive it happening (or not happening) in his own congregation. When the church grows so fast that it becomes a movement, the following two events are usually occurring:

1. The faith spreads between persons who know one another within a particular social unit.
2. It spreads from one particular social unit to another within the same subculture or homogeneous population.

If there are no Christians in a particular social unit or subculture, a movement to Christ can begin among them only when a cross-cultural communicator of the Gospel reaches across from his or her subculture, communicates the great news in a form that is indigenous to the receiving people, and wins one or several converts from among the most receptive members. These then proceed to evangelize members of their own social unit and their own subculture. The *most* contagion takes place within the existing social networks of credible Christians as they reach out to friends, relatives, fellow workers, and neighbors.

The bridges-of-God pattern is demonstrated in the New Testament. When Andrew discovers that Jesus is the promised Messiah, he turns spontaneously to his brother Simon with this good news (John 1). When the possessed man in chains is liberated, Jesus said to him, "Go home to your friends, and tell them how much the Lord has done for you, and how he has had mercy on you" (Mark 5:19). Throughout the book of Acts, two strategies seem to be paramount: (1) the missionary to a new community first identified the most receptive particular population in that community—frequently the Gentile "God fearers" who

31

attended meetings at the local church synagogue, and proclaimed the Gospel to them;[4] (2) upon winning some converts in that target population, they then reached out to all the persons within their social web. By those two strategies, the missionaries were able to raise up in quite measurable time a self-propagating indigenous church and move on to another community to start the process all over again.

What a web movement of the Christian faith looks like was spelled out in a recent issue of *Church Growth Bulletin*.[5] The great growth of a church in Taiwan began when the pastor, the Reverend Lee, visited in the hospital a Mr. Hwang, who accepted the Christian faith and asked for and received baptism, and shortly died. Lee led the funeral service where many relatives and friends of Mr. Hwang gathered. The widow, Mrs. Hwang, and all her children soon became Christians. A close friend attended the funeral; he and his whole family became converts. Another close friend attended the funeral, Lee visited him; he became a Christian and proceeded to evangelize the other members of his family. One evening, as he told Bible stories to his children, his own grandmother overheard the stories. There was a stirring in her depths; she became a Christian and led another grandson and a neighbor woman into the faith. That neighbor led her husband, a policeman, into the faith, who in turn evangelized his police beat partner. That second policeman led his wife, who in turn led a neighbor, who in turn led her husband and a daughter into the Christian faith, and the daughter's husband came in too, and on and on.

Just that one web movement produced a mighty growing congregation in Taiwan. The four kinds of links that provide bridges to the Christian faith—relatives, friends, neighbors, fellow workers—are all dramatized in that case study, although not necessarily in the same percentages that one would find in other web movements.

The American Pattern

Does the spread of the faith take place this way in the cultures and subcultures of the North Americn continent? It varies from people to people and culture to culture in a highly pluralistic nation like ours, but much growth occurs along the kinds of natural social bridges described above, usually more often than we realize. When American mainline churches discover how indigenous to American soil this principle is, how potent it is, and how to program outreach based on this insight, many congregations will show new apostolic growth.

For instance, the Central United Protestant Church of Richland, Washington, has shown great growth in the last eight years. The members of this church have historically put most of their eggs in the media basket, especially radio and television spots and programming. In late 1976, however, they surveyed their new members and discovered that the primary contact that attracted them to the church was Christian people in their social networks. Invitations from family members accounted for 18 percent, and invitations from friends and neighbors accounted for 48 percent. In other words, 66 percent of the new members of a media-emphasizing congregation were responding *essentially* to a Christian in *their* social web. The church leaders rightly believe that the media ministries are important outreach and are retaining them. But now they emphasize outreach across social networks more consciously and intentionally and are growing more than ever. Now 83 percent of their new members are coming by invitation from Christian friends.

National studies of converts and new members reveal that the bridges principle operates much more than we usually perceive. Three different kinds of studies should demonstrate this sufficiently.

In data of a suggestive nature, a recent Gallup survey of

churchgoers reveals that 58 percent of those who now go to church regularly, first began going when they were invited by *someone they knew.* Conversely, 63 per cent of those who do not go to church report that none of their friends or acquaintances has ever invited them.

Dr. Winfield Arn, of the Institute for American Church Growth, has interviewed or polled some four thousand converts, primarily on the American west coast. Arn wanted to know, What engages people? What are the doors of entry? His conclusions are instructive:

6% to 8%—just walked in
2% to 3%—through the church's programs
8% to 12%—the pastor attracted them
3% to 4%—came out of a special need
1% to 2%—were visited by church members
3% to 4%—came through a Sunday school class
70% to 80%—invited by relatives and friends

Arns adds, parenthetically, that less than one-tenth of 1 percent say they came to church membership as a direct result of any kind of city-wide evangelistic campaign.

Lyle R. Schaller's eighteen years of research into growing and nongrowing congregations across America provides the most extensive data base of any American church growth researcher. Several of his conclusions should be taught by every local church leader across the United States:

1. Schaller, for many years, has asked church members questions such as, "Why are you a member of *this* parish rather than some other church in this community?" He reports that "between two-thirds and three-fourths of the people give responses which can be classified as friendship or kinship ties."[6]

2. Significantly, Schaller reports that "in most rapidly growing congregations, two-thirds to seven-eights of the recent adult new members first attended at the invitations of a friend or relative."[7]

3. "Even more significant, in rapidly growing congregations, friendship ties are mentioned far more often than kinship ties. By contrast, in the declining parish, kinship ties account for a substantial number of all members, while friendship ties are rarely mentioned. The moral: the parish that seeks to grow should look at how friendship ties can be increased between individual members and persons who are not active members of any worshiping congregation."[8]

4. I would add another moral. The church must also teach its members to reach out through their already existing friendship ties. What presently happens spontaneously to produce some church grōwth will produce much more when the principle is used as a conscious strategy of the congregation.

As a Working Strategy

How can the established principle of the bridges of God be fleshed out as an informed approach to programmatic outreach through our churches? What basic guidelines are known and productive? Let us move toward several guidelines through a case study of a growing church.

Dr. McGavran tells of a Mennonite church in Japan that has been for years the fastest-growing congregation of its denomination in that land. It employs basically just this one principle of church growth, not having time to implement any others. It programs the principle in a way that is indigenous to the target population, as follows.

They give new converts "postconversion training," which is done in a one-to-one format, one evening per week for three months, in the new convert's home. The trainer invites the convert's family members to join in the training experience if they are interested, but that is just a small part of the social network strategy.

The trainer and convert spend a few minutes each

training evening listing some of the relatives, friends, fellow workers, and neighbors in the convert's social network. By the end of the three months, just about every "significant other" in the new convert's life has been identified and mapped out on paper.

The convert identifies those persons who are undiscipled, that is, are not regular followers of Jesus in any congregation. From among those names of undiscipled people, the trainer asks the convert, "Which of these people do you have some influence with?" The convert circles those names and with the trainer goes to see them. He shares what has been happening in his life and introduces his trainer who shares something of the Gospel and gives him or her a pamphlet or scripture portions. They invite the person to come to the church or to a special meeting with them. If some receptivity is expressed, the convert and trainer visit the person a number of times until he or she decides what to do with the great invitation. This Japanese Mennonite church so identifies the persons in every new convert's social network and reaches out in this way to a number of those persons. It has proven to be an amazingly productive way to structure, plan, and execute programmatic outreach through the church. Some indigenous version of that strategy could be productive for almost any church in America.

These guidelines are suggested by that case study and the earlier material:

1. The church's leaders should take ongoing initiatives in making new friendships with undiscipled persons in the community.
2. Secure the names of undiscipled persons within the social units of your active credible Christians and (especially) your new converts. Repeat this process every season. One reason why new converts can be especially reproductive is because they have many more existing social bridges to undiscipled persons than do old-established church members. And the

new convert's confession of faith to his peers will solidify his own self-image as a Christian.[9]

3. Make *lists* of undiscipled people who have been befriended by church leaders or who have been identified in the already existing social networks of your active Christians. Update those lists frequently, at least each season.

4. As you visit these persons develop a file card on each person, upon which you record particular information about the person's background, felt needs, points from conversations, and the person's degree of receptivity—receptive, interested, indifferent, resistent, or hostile. Spend the most time with the receptive and interested persons—*while* they are receptive or interested.

5. If you discover a particular social unit (or subunit), with virtually no discipled members in its ranks—reach out cross (sub)-culturally, make friends with the most receptive persons among them, win some of them and then encourage them *to win their peers in great numbers.*

6. Work to make your expression of this principle indigenous to your target population—speaking their language, engaging their felt needs, offering ministries, and inviting responses in ways that "fit" *those* people culturally.

May I say, parenthetically, that this strategy of the bridges of God shows the way to new church growth for many "small" congregations in America. When you mention "evangelizing" to leaders of small churches, they cringe, in part because their image of evangelizing is Christians reaching out to strangers and assimilating them into the small congregation. They acknowledge the importance of outreach to strangers and "know" they "ought" to do that, but cringe inwardly because most small-church members are not socially aggressive. They feel that the assimilation of "strangers" would undermine the nature of the small congregation as a single-cell church in which everyone cares and knows or knows about everyone else on a regular basis.[10]

But *that* kind of outreach is not necessary for the small church to grow. If the small church will simply identify the undiscipled persons in the community who are *already* within the social network of one or more of the active church members and reach out to *them*, the church will grow and still retain much of its special nature. Then, as you win some of those people, identify undiscipled people in *their* social network and reach out to *them*. By the links in that kind of continuing strategy, the small congregation will reach many people and grow, using and not undermining its essence as a small congregation.

This principle is best seen as a working strategy through case studies of creative congregations who have discovered or learned the principle and have adapted it to their situation. The following cases are drawn from church growth in the American "Sun-belt," but there is variety within this unity.

The Maple Avenue United Methodist Church in Marietta, Georgia, is in fast-growing Cobb County, north of Atlanta. The pastor, Don Jordan, took a church growth course at Scarritt College in 1977 and began teaching the principles to his leaders. Jordan held a wedding for an unchurched couple and befriended the bride's father, who liked Jordan, visited the church, and subsequently joined as a new believer. Two days later his neighbor's twenty-three-year-old son was killed in an automobile accident. The family had no church and no pastor, so Jordan and a layperson supported them until past 2:00 A.M. The next day other lay-people brought meals to the home and met incoming relatives at Atlanta airport with the church's van. They asked Jordan if the funeral could be held in Maple Avenue Church. This caring ministry became contagious in the people's neighborhood social network, out of which eight families soon united with the congregation, including eight of the fourteen adults on profession of first-time faith.

The congregation is experiencing unprecedented growth. Their evangelism committee, planning for the future, has discovered that of the 110,000 people who will move into Cobb County by 1990, 68 percent will be within fifteen minutes' driving of Maple Avenue Church. They have become especially effective at reaching and assimilating "working people."

The Frazer Memorial United Methodist Church, in a region of Montgomery, Alabama, is probably the fastest growing congregation in the history of Alabama Methodism, from 480 to 2,000 members in a six-year period. The members have learned "to work the bridges." A small neighborhood called Arrowhead is a case in point. One of the first three families on Arrowhead Drive joined Frazer and invited the newer neighbors two doors down, and these two families invited still other families. The church's leaders discovered that this was happening, rather spontaneously, when they made a membership placement map and were forced, on the small-scale map of Arrowhead neighborhood, to put pins on top of pins! The pastor, John Ed Matheson, had read McGavran's *Understanding Church Growth*, perceived what was happening, and taught the material to his people. What had been happening unintentionally would now be done intentionally and better. Frazer Memorial Church now has some eighty-five family units from Arrowhead, more than a third of all the neighborhood's families, and is repeating the strategy with similar effectiveness in several target neighborhoods. A great many adults join by profession of faith as new Christians—seventy-seven in 1978.

The First Baptist Church of Albuquerque, New Mexico, fashioned an indigenous version of this strategy that contains a memorable story. In a Sunday evening service, Mary, a divorcee in her early thirties, a cocktail waitress, came forward during the singing of "Just As I Am," announcing her desire to become a follower of Christ.

First Baptist Church members discovered that Mary needed to be baptized, so a service of baptism for her was scheduled for a Sunday evening several weeks later. The friend who had originally brought Mary to the church did an interesting thing. She sent out engraved invitations, like those usually sent for a graduation or wedding, to all the people in Mary's Albuquerque social network. That Sunday evening several rows were filled with her friends from the bowling alley, friends from the beauty parlor, fellow workers and friends from the cocktail lounge, neighbors, a parent, cousins, her former husband, her current boy-friend! That group surely must have represented most of her entire social network!

The pastor held a reception afterward. It was a celebration, with much singing. He briefly shared with Mary's friends what had been happening in her life. He simply offered to them the resources and ministries of that congregation, including the friendship of Christ.

For the next six Sunday evenings, Mary walked down the aisle during the singing of the invitational hymn, on these occasions bringing into the faith one or more persons out of her social web. Thus it is rumored (although I cannot document this last point) the people of that Baptist church in Albuquerque, New Mexico, were chanting "Hail Mary, full of grace!"

III

Motivating Local Church People for Church Growth

Many pastors agonize over "how to motivate church people to get with it in evangelism." Once a church has seen its mission field and has received good training and resourcing for the task, how do you awaken within church people, especially the leaders, the inner drives expressed in evangelistic ministry? One pastor of an ex-rural congregation asks: "Our church is providentially placed amid a harvest, but our people do not perceive this, or do not care. What can I do? Does the denominational agency have a game plan?"

Notice, the issue is how to motivate leaders to plan and *do* effective evangelism. Many leaders already "sympathize" with the church's evangelistic mission. They even attend evangelism conferences, read books, and thrill to stories of where evangelization is happening. They are vicariously involved, but are not actually reaching out to human beings in their community.

Now, motivating people for *anything* is complex and intimidating. So much is not known, yet there exists a jungle of ideas and contentions.

For instance, the great psychologists are divided on what *basically* motivates human beings. Freud saw survival motives as dominant; Adler saw the will to mastery or power; Frankl, meaning, Allport, altruism, Maslow, self-realization. "Theory X" contends that people are motivated by reward and punishment, so ride herd on them. But "Theory Y" contends that people have an inner desire for task completion and achievement, so enable them. The jungle is made thicker when we perceive that people do not usually act or behave out of just one motive; "Most behavior is multi-motivated" (Maslow).[1] Furthermore, some motives for acting are conscious within a person, but many are subconscious—influencing decisions and behavior in ways of which the person is not aware.

Regarding the particular question of how to motivate local church leaders for evangelism, much research still needs to be done and will require at least a modest volume. But church growth related research has uncovered enough factors upon which to build a strategy.

Back the Church's Whole Evangelistic Mission

We are becoming increasingly sure that our *goal* is to motivate the leaders to support and become appropriately involved in the *several* facets of church growth, not merely the facet that would enable their own congregation to grow numerically. Church growth scholars stress that God calls Christ's Holy Church to grow in essentially four different ways:

1. *Internal growth* is the growth in the congregation's quality or depth that is desired in addition to its numerical growth. When the people learn to pray more devoutly, become more immersed in Scripture and sacrament, more loving in their fellowship, more sensitive and obedient to the will of God for justice, peace, reconciliation, evangelization, and liberation, the church is experiencing internal growth. When inactive or nominal members experience an awakened faith and become *real* disciples, internal growth is

occurring. Internal growth is the base upon which the other ways of church growth depend. The kind of growth that Christ mandates is *both* quantitative and qualitative.

2. *Expansion growth* occurs when the congregation "expands" by bringing in new members into its ranks. This expansion growth is further subdivided: *(a) biological growth* happens when our own children from church families come up through the ranks, attend Sunday school, confirmation training, and join the church on confession of faith; *(b) transfer growth* happens when a church member joins another congregation; *(c) conversion growth* happens when previously undiscipled people join the church, for the first time, on confession of faith. This kind of expansion is even more important than the others. *Outreach for conversion growth is the towering priority of the evangelistic congregation.*

3. *Extension growth* occurs when the congregation (usually in cooperation with its judicatory) reaches people whom that congregation cannot reach, because of geographical and/or cultural distance, by starting a new congregation with ministries especially indigenous to the target population. Mobile middle-Americans and the new floods of immigrant peoples, especially Hispanic and Asian, provide an opportunity for a renaissance in extension growth.

4. *Bridging growth* occurs when the church is planted by new cross-cultural evangelization among significantly different cultures and tongues from that of the "sending" church, populations usually geographically removed as well. Although it is fashionable in some quarters to say that "the sending of missionaries is now outmoded" and is "not where the action is," in fact there are over 2.7 billion unreached people in the world, a greater number than ever before, who live in people units with no Christians in their ranks. New Christian movements can only be started in these people units by the sending of cross-cultural communicators of the Gospel, servants of Christ needed in

unprecedented numbers. Some of these will be Asian and African, but many must be from the numerous and affluent denominations of Europe and America.

Now, three points are relevant in this discussion. First, many church leaders want expansion growth without bothering with internal growth. But this denies expansion growth the ever-wider and deeper base that it needs. Most new people won into such a church are not assimilated into the group life and ministries of the congregation and are quickly lost to the inactive status.

Second, many leaders count on expansion growth by biological and transfer growth alone without outreach to undiscipled populations. This betrays the heart of the Great Commission. While such a church in a fortunate setting may experience numerical growth for awhile, the policy contributes to long-term stagnation for the Christian mission.

Third, many leaders are interested in expansion growth for their congregation (and perhaps internal growth) but turn a deaf ear to Christ's mandate for extension growth and bridging growth. Such congregations, more interested in building their institution than in reaching *all* people, reach out to the people their church can get to, and forget the rest. We have reasons to believe that our Lord *refuses to affirm and empower* the outreach efforts of a congregation primarily motivated by institutional selfishness whether the efforts are of congregational or denominational scope.

This is perhaps the main reason why some churches and denominations who have "gotten into church growth" (that is, attended seminars, read the books, set goals, and begun informed outreach ministries) *have not experienced* the new apostolic contagion they thought they were promised. When a church twists Wesley's bold "The World Is My Parish" into "My Parish Is My World," God absents himself. That is why Kenneth Chafin can declare, "Show me a denomination that has stopped planting new congregations, and I'll show you a denomination that is already in a terminal condition." So *the whole enterprise* needs strong motivation supporting and energizing its several thrusts.

Some Traditional Approaches Not Recommended

The necessity of motivating church people for evangelism is not, of course, unique to this generation. Many times the leaders of previous generations have motivated laypeople effectively, and the principles we will commend in the next sections are, in part, historically informed. But some inherited motivational appeals cannot be recommended:

1. *Guilt*. Frequently pastors have rebuked church people, inducing feelings of strong guilt for who they are not, and for what they are not doing. Such an appeal can crank up some activity for awhile, long enough to reduce the guilt feelings to a tolerable level, but it is not an effective long-term strategy. Lyle E. Schaller, from his twenty years of studying congregations, contends that

> Perhaps the most effective means of creating *passivity* in a congregation is to use guilt as the basic motivating force. While this may enable the congregation to achieve ambitious goals and it often produces a large amount of surface activity, eventually it takes its toll. The Christian Church is based on the love of God for His children and the use of guilt as a motivating tool runs counter to that basic theme. In some congregations it may take a generation for the full sequence to become visible, but guilt usually leads first to agitated activity followed next by hostility and finally by passivity.[2]

2. *Duty*. Even more frequently, pastors appeal to people's sense of duty, exhorting them in regard to what they ought to do. This is an impotent appeal; people agree but do not act. I observed a pastor exhorting his eleven o'clock congregation to "pick up prospect cards on the way

out and make three visits to unchurched people on the way home. This is your duty." The following message was written across the faces of the people, "Yeah, we ought to do that, but we're going straight home before the roast burns."

3. *Eternal Reward.* Sometimes church people are promised "a star in your crown" if they will win someone to the faith. Mormon proselytizing is primarily based on the promise of eternal reward in proportion to the number of converts one secures. This motive appeal, while it may be "successful" for some, is unworthy of Christian evangelism. We are called to evangelize because we will the best for other persons, not because we want something more for ourselves.

Recommended Approaches to Motivating: Theological

As we now focus on motivational strategies and appeals that we *can* recommend, one principle should be foremost in church growth planning. We identify a number of principles. Do not employ just one, but *many*. If Abraham Maslow is right, that "most behavior is multi-motivational," then the local evangelism leader's task is to awaken or introduce several motives in each leader and harness and direct those for actual evangelism planning and ministries. So, ride all or most of the following motivational appeals frequently.

1. Gratitude to Christ

Canon Michael Green, in his classic *Evangelism in the Early Church*, reports that great hosts of first- and second-century rank-and-file Christians evangelized

> because of the overwhelming experience of the love of God which they had received through Jesus Christ. The discovery that the ultimate force in the universe was Love, and that this love had stooped to the very nadir of self-abasement for human good, had an effect on those who believed it which nothing can remove.[3]

Green adds that "reflection upon the cross as the supreme impulse of costly service for others in the name of the gospel was unquestionably the greatest single element in keeping the zeal of Christians at fever pitch."[4]

Gratitude to Christ is probably the greatest single theological factor in the leader's motives in growing congregations today. So proclaim the kind of Gospel and help create the kind of experiences that enable people to experience the transforming grace and love of God. People who have recently experienced this Reality, for the first time or afresh, will be among your motivated evangelizers.

2. Obedience to the Great Commission

Upon the "rock" of faith in Christ, he created and continued to build his Church. The Great Commission to go . . . make disciples among all peoples is the banner pointing the way for the expansion of his Body and its ministry and mission. Since the Great Commission appears in several different forms in the New Testament, some have thought that there is room for speculation on what exactly was said by Jesus. But the fact of its several different versions in the Gospels and Epistles reveal it to be at the heart of the apostolic Church's self-understanding, a reason for the resolute new-disciple-making outreach, which that Church preaches and dramatizes throughout the book of Acts.

The Church exists as Christ's Body, extending his mission to all lost, hurting, oppressed peoples. As Roland Allen stressed, the Great Commission is not a "legal" command that one obeys in some kind of "Christian legalism." It is rather Christ's announcement of our identity. We accept the Commission as a privilege, to join him in the Way he is leading. Churches that accept this offered privilege and have their priorities straight are free to experience apostolic growth.

47

3. Love for Neighbor

The title of C. B. Hogue's book, *Love Leaves No Choice: Lifestyle Evangelism* (Waco: Word Books, 1976), suggests the heartbeat of this motive. Church leaders who compassiontely will the best for people are needed in great numbers. Leaders who *want* lost people found, estranged people reconciled, and defeated people empowered are motivated to reach out to them.

This motive rooted in *agape*-love is prominent in every generation of great Christian disciple-making evangelization. Origen's ancient test of this motive, while hyperbolic, is inescapable today: "Do you have sorrow and grief for the lost? Do you *care enough* to be separated from Christ for them?"[5]

4. The Conviction That Christ Is with Us

Christ is present in the world, awakening by his "prevenient grace" receptivity in many people. He calls us to join him in this outreach as his ambassadors, through whom he can articulate his appeal. He promises to empower us, even to give us the words that fit particular circumstances. When Christians become convinced that Christ himself is leading and is with them, nothing can stop them.

As an evangelism/church growth consultant in congregations, I frequently ask in a leader's meeting, "What are you now attempting in your mission which would only succeed if God were with you?" In growing churches the leaders are able to offer several spontaneous answers. In stagnant churches the leaders become temporarily mute.

Recommended Approaches to Motivating: Practical

1. Get leaders involved with the facts.
Church growth consultants in North America have repeatedly discovered the subtle motivating power of

involving key leaders with the facts and data relevant to their congregation's mission. Such knowledge is also necessary for the congregation's accurate perception of its mission field, history, and strengths and for good planning based on sound factual knowledge.

The leaders need the facts about their community, or ministry, area. For instance, a United Methodist Church in Donelson, Tennessee, assumed it could not grow because of the dominant image in the community of a fast-growing Baptist church nearby, a bellwether church of the Southern Baptist Convention. But the Methodists discovered that that church has "only" thirty-two hundred members out of a population of sixty-five thousand, that about half of the sixty-five thousand are not regularly involved in anyone's church, and that several "kinds of people," usually reachable by Methodists, are not being effectively engaged by the Baptist church or by anyone else. The Methodist congregation, armed with these facts, began to see the possibilities that its previously uninformed assumptions had eclipsed.

Leaders need to see *their church* afresh. Things are almost never the way people "remember" them. For instance, a return visit to the home you spent a summer in as a child will jar you into perceiving that it is not, and was not, as you "remembered" it. To help your leaders perceive *and become involved* with the church's facts employ the widely tested exercise that Dr. McGavran delineates in the next chapter.

2. *As you recruit members for ministries, give them a terminal date.*

Many church members have already been burned by accepting church roles or tasks that turned out to be implied lifetime contracts which, when they later asked to be relieved of the responsibility, were made to feel guilty. They are not eager to approach that fire again. But a clear terminal contract can help motivate many of them for new involvement, especially if several motivational forces are already working within them.

49

For instance, the late Dr. George Fallon, founding pastor of a new congregation in Arlington, Texas, built from scratch a program of visitation evangelism using this method. He asked members for a nine-month commitment to visit undiscipled prospects once a week whenever they were free on a visiting night. As many as were schedule-free visited the first Monday, second Tuesday, third Wednesday, and fourth Thursday of each month for the nine months. He discovered three advantages to this plan: (*a*) more members, at least much of the time, were involved than would have been in a plan for visiting the same night each week; (*b*) they found more people at home on *some* week night than they would have in visiting just one week night; (*c*) many members who might not have responded to an open-ended appeal were psychologically free to commit themselves for nine months.

The specified period might be considerably different than the above nine-month suggestion. The Reverend Gene Nease of a growing church in Tulsa, Oklahoma, joins his evangelism leaders in asking for eighteen-week commitments to visit one night each week. At the end of the eighteen weeks, their commitment *ends*. They *may* recommit for another period. Some stay in, some do not, some come back later.

3. *Provide social support for those involved in evangelistic ministry.*

Psychologically speaking, many of the ministries of evangelism are "threatening." Many laypeople cringe at the prospect of reaching out, exclaiming, "anything but that." And, at least in mainline denominations, the rate of people who try it and retreat to the encampment is quite high. Part of the reason for such a regrettable outcome is lack of social support in three aspects.

First, those members involved in outreach must receive the widespread and repeated affirmation and recognition of the congregation. They need the sign that what they are engaged in, with some rigor and risk, is supremely

50

important. But if the congregation pays more attention to the church officers and those involved in maintenance rather than outreach, that communicates what the congregation thinks is really important and fails to adequately support outreach. In addition, the church's evangelizers need the prayer support of the congregation and its groups and classes.

Second, those engaged in actual outreach to undiscipled people need to meet regularly in support of one another before and after going to visit. Their koinonia will provide both *esprit de corps* and situational learning, much like the huddle of a football team before and after each involvement from the scrimmage line.

Third, make sure that some of your most attractive, energetic, natural leaders are involved in evangelistic outreach. Not only do some of those people make your best evangelizers, but their presence in the "huddle" and the outreach will be an incentive to some other members to become involved.

4. *Give people current feedback.*

A negative example may clarify this principle. One pastor, each January, writes evaluation notes to each worker in the church who has done something the previous year. That is all right, but for some workers the evaluation will be received nine or ten months too late.

People need more rapid evaluation of their performance in church roles and tasks. If they start out right, this merits reinforcing. If they begin by steering a wrong course, the leader needs to intervene and change that course while people are still educable and before the behavior has been engrained in personality by much repetition and defended because of long ego-investment.

5. *Involve each member in a task for which he or she has gifts.*

People are motivated to make a contribution when they are invited to do something for which they have a gift(s) of

51

creation and/or the Spirit.[6] Within the total program of the church's evangelistic outreach, identify the tasks that need doing and match people appropriately. A rather representative list of the needed tasks would look like the following:

1. Keep records and prospect files
2. Survey community
3. Make friendly visits in homes
* 4. Participate in evangelistic conversations
* 5. Counsel receptive people for possible commitment
6. Train new members
7. Sponsor new members
8. Assimilate new members into group life
9. Assimilate new members into roles and tasks
10. Participate in various tasks of advocacy, evaluation, planning, promotion, and publicity for the congregation's evangelism program.

Naturally, evangelistic conversation and counseling (*4 and *5) are crucial and central tasks, calling for the following special strategy.

Identify *Members* with the *Gift* of *Evangelism*

Some members need to be involved in those special kinds of transactions in which the great news is shared and a response is encouraged and enabled. Regarding all the tasks of programmatic evangelism, but especially the central task of communicating for conversion, three basic points need to be registered.

First, *you cannot motivate* everyone in the congregation to participate in evangelism. Some members, for whatever reasons, will *never* evangelize; others will remain magnificently obsessed with some other ministry in God's work. So, do not wait until everyone is motivated and on board in evangelism before you plan and reach out.

Second, some of your people are *already* motivated, and gifted, for some ministry of evangelism. A survey of your people will reveal that motives conducive to evangelism are already present in many people. Simply and clearly offer to people the opportunity to become involved in ministries for which they are already motivated and gifted.

Third, among those who are motivated or motivatable choose those who have the "gift of the Spirit" for evangelizing (tasks 4 and 5 above).[6]

Now, *how do you know* which members have the gifts to be the church's avocational evangelizers? Well, you do not ask for volunteers. Because some persons who think they have it, do not; other persons who have barely dreamed they have it, do. The *leaders*, using their gift of discernment, perceive who has the gift and recruit them.

There are clues, or criteria, for helping the leaders perceive the members who most likely have the gifts to be evangelizers. The author has consistently observed that six guidelines are virtually always useful, and three others are frequently helpful.

What to Look for in Searching for Evangelizers

1. Look for *convinced Christians*, not necessarily doctrinaire or cocky Christians, but Christians who are in touch with Christian Reality. They know Christ, they experience grace, they find discipleship in the community of faith to be deeply meaningful.
2. Look for Christians who *believe in the importance* of evangelistic outreach. For them, the Great Commission is not an option or merely one-among-many wishes of our Lord. It is supremely important that all persons and peoples have the opportunity to know Christ and become his followers.
3. Look for Christians *who can listen.* Effective interpersonal

evangelism is about four-fifths listening and one-fifth talking. So, eliminate obsessional chatterers, persons who express their nervousness by talking *ad nauseam,* and Christians who itch to tell and retell their spiritual autobiography. Choose potentially good listeners and teach them those known skills that inform effective listening.

4. Look for Christians who can *empathize,* who, in their listening, *feel with* another person and *identify* with that person's pain and struggle. This capacity for incarnational love is indispensable.

5. Look for Christians who are *articulate.* Do not look for glibness or eloquence, which could be counter-productive among many prospective Christians. But do recruit Christians who can accurately and clearly verbalize: what they perceive of the other person's pain, struggle, search, or situation, and the facet(s) of the Gospel especially relevant to that person's felt needs.

6. Freely select potential outreachers on the basis of the five guidelines above. Later, after say six months to a year of the Christian's new ministry-in-outreach, impose another guideline question, Has the Holy Spirit certified this Christian's early outreach ministry? Has any person been attracted into or toward Christian discipleship since this Christian started reaching out? If negative, then earlier perceptions about this Christian's gift for evangelism may have been inaccurate. Guide him/her into some other ministry of the Church.

Other helpful guidelines: 1. As the congregation's leaders discern gifts among the members to determine who has the gift for evangelizing, the quality of *patience* ought not to be overlooked. Virtually no one becomes a Christian in one transaction the first time anyone ever opens up the

Possibility to them, so your evangelizers should not expect to see many instant Christians. It takes weeks or months for the majority of persons to work through the process of adopting the faith and becoming disciples and members of the Body. Evangelizers must be sensitive and patient enough to cooperate with God's time (*kairos*) and not push their time (*chronos*).

2. As you send Christians out to evangelize, you will usually want to match evangelizers with persons with whom there is "homogeneity," a sense of cultural common bond. For instance, send out a physician to a physician, an athlete to an athlete, a middle-class Korean-American to a middle-class Korean-American, a member from "back East" to a new resident from Pennsylvania. Exceptions to this normal principle could be exercised in cases where the evangelizer is a skilled cross-cultural communicator, or the receptor is significantly melted, assimilated, upwardly mobile in aspirations, or for some other reason, is in a position to receive and hear someone significantly different from him.

3. New converts will make up a disproportionate number of your evangelizers. They have the contagion of a recent discovery. They still have many friends who are undiscipled, and they still speak the language of ordinary secular people. Extensive church growth research teaches that new converts will be much more reproductive (as a group and with some exceptions) than long-time established Christians. And, in general, first-generation Christians make more effective evangelizers than second-, third-, and fourth-generation Christians.

4. In stressing the role of the leaders in discerning the gifts of the members and recruiting evangelizers, this is not a unilateral or authoritarian process. The leaders should teach the members about the ministries of the laity and the biblical concept of gifts for ministry. They should encourage

the members to discover their own gifts and to report their belief that they might have the gift for evangelizing. Peter Wagner's well-known "five steps toward discovering your spiritual gift" are instructive:[7] (a) explore the possibilities, (b) experiment with as many as you can, (c) examine your feelings, (d) evaluate your effectiveness, (e) expect confirmation from the Body. These steps for the *members* to take are congruent with the above prescribed steps for the *leaders* to take. Leaders and members are called to join in the mutual simultaneous quest to discover and deploy the gift(s) for ministry of every member. My own stress is upon the discernment and recruiting initiatives of the congregation's leaders. The perception of the leaders should be corroborated by the subjective experience of the member, and a member's sense of being gifted should be corroborated by the discernment of the leaders.

The Congregational Climate for an Outreach-Motivated People

Motivation does not take place in a vacuum but in the social-spiritual setting of the congregation's life. Certain factors in that congregational life can produce a "climate" conducive to church growth motivation. And, like planting cotton in the Dakotas, if the climate is not conducive to growth, neither growth nor the motivation for it is likely to be generated.

1. One indispensable factor is strong, indigenous, utterly celebrative congregational worship. The congregation emerges in contagious outreach from a worship life that is enjoyed, where the Gospel and Christ's vision for humanity is communicated and trumpeted, where the grace of God and exciting fellowship with fellow believers are experienced.

Also, the worship must engage visitors. The members must be spontaneously and genuinely welcoming and friendly; the visitor must feel comfortable and wanted. The liturgy and the preaching must be in the dialect and heart language of the people the church wants to reach. And the hymnody must be of a genre to which the target population can resonate; it must "fit" them culturally.

The visitor regards the eleven o'clock worship service as a shopwindow revealing the church's goods, services, and identity. That shopwindow must be engaging. If it is not, most visitors will leave to look in other windows.

And if it is not engaging, the members will know it and will not be motivated to invite their friends and acquaintances to church. Many mainline congregations are still fairly full of members who show up out of habit, or duty, or friendships in the church, but do not feel the worship to be enough of a credible or magnetic event to warrant inviting others to it.

2. Through pulpit, classroom, and other media, the church must convey to members the deep and sustained conviction that reaching people and making new disciples is supremely important. The Great Commission is the Magna Charta of this congregation. And everything else we want to do for people and this community through our multiple ministries is dependent on a growing number of new disciples to become the personnel for those ministries. Indeed, growth in this mission field is the congregation's destiny and Christ himself is present and is calling us to fulfill this loving mandate. "Love leaves no choice."

The conveying of this conviction is more than an instructional task. It will be conveyed to a greater extent through, and as a by-product of, the people's beginning involvements with evangelism activities. Indeed, some behavioral involvement is usually a prerequisite to the flowering of a strong motivation within people, so do not plan to motivate people first and then get them involved. It is *as* they participate in contagious worship, meet new converts filled with life, plan for church growth, back outreach with their money, and take first attempts at sharing the Gospel-possibility, that *strong* motivation will *follow*, which will in turn empower the congregation's greater and more sustained apostolic achievement.

IV

Training the Laity for Church Growth

Before we can talk intelligently about training the laity, we must assess the times in which we live. Do we train in the midst of a vast security or in a shaken world? Can we assume that the Church is always going to be here? Are we training the laity in a rapidly growing Church or one which is resting on its laurels? I maintain that training must be done in dangerous times, in the midst of extremely rapid social change facing many declining mainline and evangelical churches. We cannot be good stewards of the grace of God without fitting our training to a radically rearranged set of priorities. Today, growth training is not merely a nice thing to do. It is urgent.

It is difficult for Americans to believe the danger. We have been a secure people. The Church has seemed strong and impregnable. The American way of life has stood like the Rock of Gibraltar. Who could shake it? This nation has not been invaded. We have not been conquered. Our Gross National Product continues to rise. Our farms produce more and more. Our education is good. Larger and larger parts of our population are becoming truly free and are rising above the poverty level. Blacks are treated better. Beautiful churches, set on five-acre plots of choice land, are found in all cities. Seminary complexes worth millions of dollars are found in almost every state. With all this, it is hard to believe that the Church stands in any real danger, or that it will not be able to do what its Master directs.

Yet we shall not see the urgency and utter necessity of training the laity for growth unless we discern the grave dangers facing us. The fact of the matter is that we train the laity not in the midst of flower-flecked fields, beside still waters, but in an earthquake with walls tumbling down all around us.

Leaders of the Church in Europe constantly speak of living in a post-Christian age. The Roman Catholic Church counts great sections of France as "mission territory," because the population is so slightly Christian. Only 5 percent of the populations of Sweden, Germany, and England worship God. American sociologists point out that the Church has not been comfortable with the city or successful in it. The city is where we lose Christians, not where we gain them. Jacques Ellul wonders whether the demonic city will triumph over the Church. The charge that the Church is irrelevant to the modern mind is commonly leveled and seldom effectively combated. Television lures as many viewers as it can, by whatever means it may, and forms the American mind more effectively than the Sunday school and the pulpit combined. The sexual revolution is a euphemism for a disastrous defeat of Christian standards. It is a rare Christian family that has not lost one or more of its loved ones to the world.

When we look within, we see many denominations that have ceased growing. Even after becoming aroused by the church growth movement, some have continued to decline. During the last decade five denominations, becoming concerned about their static condition, resolved to reverse the trend and to start growing again. I wish I could report that they are healthily growing, but I cannot. They are still barely holding their own.

At an advanced church growth seminar, nine leaders of the Reformed Church in America, one of the outstanding denominations of this land, interviewed me. One of their questions was this, *Can* a middle-class ethnic church like ours grow? They thought, quite correctly, that it would not be easy. Some of them thought it was not even possible. Training the laity for church growth is not training them to mow the lawn or to drive the freeways. Rather, it is training them in a field where success is not assured.

Perhaps the most frightening aspect of the world scene is the drift, within the Church, away from the theological certainties that in the past have always been necessary for church growth. In the past, churches with steel convictions have grown. Those with rubber convictions have declined. Dean M. Kelley draws attention to this in his provocative book, *Why Conservative Churches Are Growing.*[1] And the spread of rubber convictions is rapid. In great areas of the Church I can discern no end to the process. It is quite useless, of course, to transmit rubber convictions to lay Christians and expect them to produce anything by way of church growth.

Mainline churches, with their glorious heritage of biblical certainty, intense assurance of salvation, whitehot passion for evangelism, ought not to have much difficulty with religious relativism, universalism, and other forms of latitudinarianism; but these deviations are popular and appear in the guise of reasonable modern forms of the Christian faith, which can be held without betraying it. Thus they gather followers, erode biblical certainty, and multiply rubber convictions.

Am I suggesting a crash program for survival? No, not really. I like the sense of urgency those words convey, but would not myself use them. Mind you, I know the Old Testament repeatedly shows that when God's people disobey God's commands, *they do not survive*. Nevertheless, I do not advocate church growth in order to survive.

61

Christians act for higher motives than that. I advocate training the laity as a crash program to meet desperate human need and obey God's Word. If we would obey God and serve our fellowmen holistically (*soul* as well as body) in these times of great crisis and rapid social change, we must train Christians to achieve church growth.

How Many Laypeople Are We Talking About?

I cannot exaggerate the part lay Christians play in the growth of the Church. Unless lay Christians vigorously back it, growth does not happen. The minister can do something, but unless there is massive lay participation little growth results. How many of the laity should be trained? Let me set three views before you.

1. Some twenty years ago Kenneth Strachan formed and popularized this theorem: "The expansion of any movement is in direct proportion to its success in mobilizing its total membership in continuous propagation of its beliefs. This alone is the key."

Strachan was talking about ordinary Christians, factory workers, housewives, office workers, lawyers, politicans, physicians, business people, realtors, teachers, men and women, boys and girls. He said to mobilize them *all*. It is hard to exaggerate the potential of Christians, all engaged in continuous propagation of their beliefs.

2. Recenty C. Peter Wagner noted that on the Day of Pentecost the twelve apostles constituted exactly 10 percent of the 120 gathered for prayer in the Upper Room. He also observed that in the average American congregation, 10 percent of the membership would constitute a sizable evangelistic task force. Ten percent of those gathered at most services would mean dozens actively evangelizing their cities. Wagner then noted that when the Bible sets forth the gifts that God gives to Christians, it mentions specifically "the gift of evangelism." It is easy to conclude

that in the average American church God has given to about one in every ten the gift of evangelism. If these multitudes use their gift, churches will experience a new magnitude of growth. The principle of one-tenth has given hundreds of American congregations a goal to reach. Suppose each congregation had a tenth of its members out starting class meetings, calling, inviting, distributing tracts, conducting home Bible studies, pastoring branch churches, surveying to see where new congregations could be started.

3. I answer the question of how many laypersons should be trained by encouraging churches to divide all their unpaid volunteer workers in two categories—class-one leaders and class-two leaders. Class-one leaders serve the existing church. They teach Sunday school and are ushers and deacons. They sing in the choir and serve on the session. They are wonderful people. They make the church the delightful place it is. Class-two leaders are volunteer workers heading out away from the church. They call on those who are not members. They keep asking how depressed or oppressed segments of the population can be helped. They survey the neighborhoods to find those who seldom worship God. They start house churches and keep them going for years. They talk to secularists about Christ.

Do you see these two classes of leaders? Every healthy church ought to have about as many class-two as class-one leaders. I suggest you count them. Many churches have fifty class-ones and only a few class-twos. That is a sinful proportion. It is not pleasing to God. It seldom leads a church to find the lost in any but the smallest numbers.

In training lay Christians remember that the task force should be composed of all ranks: women, young people, men, senior citizens, wealthy and ordinary members of the congregation, black, and white. God gives gifts of evangelism to all alike as he pleases. Furthermore, all these classes and more are found in the unchurched community. To reach them, their kind of people need to be the messengers.

63

It is of particular importance that the task force be composed of a higher percent of recent converts than their numbers in the congregation would warrant. The Christian faith flows along lines of contact. Christians present the faith convincingly to friends and relatives. If those casually interested in Christ are to be transformed into enthusiastic followers, they must be grafted into the Body. That means hours and days of friendship and fellowship.

Edward Murphy conducted many evangelistic campaigns in the cities of Latin America. Many came forward and confessed Christ; but when three years later he did a careful survey to discover how the churches had grown, he found that the downtown churches had not grown at all, while the barrio churches on the edges of the city had increased considerably. Why? In the downtown churches those who came to the evangelistic meeting were people off the streets, who were unknown to the congregation. In the barrios those who came were invited by friends, intimates, and close relatives. Converts in the downtown churches were, of course, urged to come for instruction and fellowship, but lacking friends there, they seldom came. Converts in the barrio congregations were visited by friends and *brought* to the follow-up meetings. They were invited to meals. There was rejoicing at the return of the prodigal. Fatted calves were killed. Naturally converts were transformed into responsible members.

New converts are of key importance, because they have been recently in the world. Most of their friends are in the world. When trained in evangelism, they have many contacts. Andrew finds his brother Simon and brings him to Jesus.

A corollary of the principle I have been setting forth is that starting a stream of new converts flowing into the church is more difficult than keeping that stream flowing. In the beginning, a church has to use seasoned Christians who have very few contacts in the world. As soon as growth starts, these long-time Christians ought to be supplemented by as many young Christians as possible. New converts should be trained for church growth.

Pastors will find it rewarding to analyze their evangelistic task force from the above point of view. If you have no one but seasoned Christians, thank God for them and go ahead, but as soon as you can get new Christians, encourage many of them (far more than 10 percent of them) to train for evangelism.

If you can mobilize your whole membership for evangelism, that is splendid. Get everyone to study church growth and pray for it, but do not be surprised if you get only one in ten actually going out to do something about it. Increase the task force until you have as many class-two leaders as class-ones and encourage them to put in more person-hours a week.

Motivate People to Enroll for Training

Let us suppose that evangelism has been neglected in a church. The pastor has done something, of course. Meetings for the deepening of the spiritual life have occurred once or twice a year, but effective evangelism has been notable by its absence. How does that church turn around? How does it get a tenth of the women, men, and young people *out evangelizing* week after week? How does a church start evangelizing?

If you simply call for volunteers, you are not likely to get many, particularly the Christians who have a gift of evangelism and do not know it. The first step may be preaching a series of sermons explaining what the Bible says about the Gospel, the lostness of people without Christ, the absolute necessity of belief in Christ, the normalcy of witness, and the joy of sharing Christ. Tell your congregation how leaders of your tradition have evangelized. If you are Methodist, describe the way in

65

which the Methodist Movement through a mighty multiplication of reborn men and women saved England from a revolution such as France experienced. Read Wesley's *Journal* until his fire burns in your soul. *Constantly speak about evangelism as a normal Christian activity.* Constantly view the surrounding populations from the point of view of church growth. In all your *prepared prayers* insert sections dealing with people's utter need for saving faith in Christ. Teach your lay leaders to pray fervently for church growth. Plead with God to grant his Holy Spirit, so that the hungry multitudes may be fed the Bread of Heaven and the famine of the Word of God ended.

With the field prepared in this fashion, show a church growth or evangelism film to the congregation. Be sure your trustees and leaders are there. As soon as the lights go up, announce that a class on church growth will be started. Each member will study a book on church growth, a chapter a week. The class will discuss what in that chapter applies to the local situation. Enroll the class right after the film. The joint study will take two or three months and will generate confidence in what can be done. At the end of the study period, you will have a task force of men and women who are ready to put in several hours a week at basic sensitive evangelism.

Some pastors may wish to institute training classes in some particular mode of evangelism. Evangelism Explosion and Campus Crusade are two well-known para-church methods. Most denominations produce usable resources, such as the Southern Baptist WIN program, and the United Methodist "Visitation Evangelism: a Relational Ministry."

Training the members of the task force is a continuous process. It is not something done with some book once and then terminated. The pastor observes how the task force is functioning and feeds in remedial training.

One of the most dramatically growing churches in the whole world is the Full Gospel Church of Yoido Island, Seoul, Korea. Its members now number fifty-six thousand and rising. It holds four worship services each Sunday: eight to ten, ten to twelve, twelve to two, and two to four. Ten thousand Christians attend each service. All this growth has been achieved in the last twelve years. Pastor Paul Yongg Cho told me, when I preached there, that converts are won, not in the church, but in the twenty-four hundred house churches in which this huge congregation meets. These twenty-four hundred house churches are led by lay Christians, more than half of them women. The twenty-four hundred are unpaid volunteer workers. Each looks after his or her congregation of twenty to thirty men and women, instructs them, sees that they get to church, visits them when they are sick and prays with them. These lay Christians are, Pastor Cho told me, essential to the growth of the church.

He meets these leaders every Wednesday afternoon at the central church on Yoido Island for three hours of instruction and inspiration. Training lay leaders goes on fifty-two weeks a year. No wonder the church grows. Note that the Full Gospel Church trains about one in twenty-three, not one in ten.

Note also that the Full Gospel Church is growing chiefly among the native-born South Koreans, whereas the great growth of both the Presbyterians and the Methodists took place among the North Koreans (before the division of the country, of course) and more recently among the refugees from North Korea who streamed into South Korea. *When laymen are properly taught and inspired, they make the church grow in populations that until then had appeared unresponsive.* I rather think that Christians with church growth eyes will cease talking about indifferent and unresponsive populations. Instead they will talk about populations in which native-born, trained, lay Christians are not working.

67

Hold a Goal-Setting Workshop

Goal setting is an ancient and honorable practice. Many achievements recorded in Scripture, such as the building of Solomon's Temple and Nehemiah's Wall, would have been impossible without it. Goal setting is also a natural and inevitable part of life; we do it in one form or another everyday.

This ancient and natural practice that God requires has been highlighted recently by the developing science of management. You can stumble into goal setting or you can use it skillfully. You can drift or set a specific course and hold tenaciously to it despite storm and adversity. Management teaches people to whom God has given responsibility for the direction of a faculty, farm, factory, or a church to set goals, which hold the whole team together. Management tells us how to sell these goals to everyone concerned, so that each person on the team owns the goal and does not feel that it is imposed. At Fuller Theological Seminary we have a Ten-Year Plan. That means we have set for ourselves annual, triennial, and ten-year goals.

Setting church growth goals is a sensible, devout, and rewarding experience, and we know more about it than ever before. It shows what is possible and what is God's will under given circumstances. It helps a congregation act in a systematic fashion. It carries the congregation along with its leader. It lays down a policy that will hold the center of the stage for the coming three years. It keeps the congregation from flitting from this enthusiasm to that. If you want your church to be a good steward of God's grace, lead it to set goals in church growth. Our warrant for suggesting this is no less than recent *global* experience.

In 1973 Virgil Gerber published an enormously influential little book on goal setting called *God's Way to Keep a Church Going and Growing*.[2] Since that time, the book has been translated into thirty-two languages. Using this book, Dr.

Gerber has organized and led church growth workshops in fifty-six countries. Since each workshop has pulled in representative pastors from the leading denominations in that land, Dr. Gerber has created a church growth conscience in denominations and congregations all around the globe. This meteoric surge of growth has happened, not during the last sixty years, but in the last six.

In country after country and denomination after denomination, pastors who had been content to shepherd their flocks have suddenly become men searching for and finding lost sheep. Laymen in thousands of congregations have become concerned about the nongrowth in their churches and have started doing something about it. Sometimes a single congregation would start growing. Sometimes a cluster of congregations and sometimes a whole denomination would enter on a period of growth. Dr. Gerber's remarkable ministry has been a dramatic demonstration of the fact that goal setting can be of major value to ordinary churches in almost any culture.

The Venezuelan experiment that started this tremendous expansion in church growth convictions was held in April, 1972. There Spanish-speaking pastors of ordinary churches brought records (some of them woefully inadequate) of their membership during the past ten years. Drs. Gerber and Wagner then taught them how to analyze, chart, and understand the growth that had, and had *not* taken place. Working with their own figures and studying those of their fellow pastors, they saw what was really happening. They provided a background of reality. They were talking about their own problems and tasks. They were not reacting against someone else's judgment, but simply seeing the real situation. In that setting, Dr. Gerber described church growth principles, knowing that his listeners would see them as "something that *we* need."

The next step was to ask participants on the basis of their past experience and in an attitude of faith and prayer to project the growth they believed God was calling them to attempt. "What do you believe God is going to give you by way of church growth?" they were asked.

The fourth step was to calculate what the average rates of growth during the last ten years had been and during the coming five years would be.

On the basis of the Venezuela experiment, Dr. Gerber prepared his now-famous book *God's Way to Keep a Church Going and Growing*. It tells in beautifully clear fashion how any group of pastors or lay Christians can hold a church growth workshop. With the book, any congregation, summer conference, or weekend retreat can do it. It helps, of course, if the leader has been through a workshop led by Dr. Gerber, but that is not necessary. In Nigeria, a missionary, Gerald Swank, got hold of an English version of the book and by himself, without ever attending a workshop, led a group of forty Nigerian pastors through the process of reporting ten-year membership, analyzing, charting, and understanding the growth that had taken place, and in faith projecting the growth they thought God wished them to have in the next five years.

One of the strengths of the book is that the first two chapters are devoted to a biblical exposition of church growth. They show how it is inherent in the Christian faith itself, how our Lord desires his lost sons and daughters found, and how beneficial it is to the world for the Body of Christ to grow. Thus, before numbers of members are mentioned, those attending the workshop have been thoroughly exposed to the view that healthy churches grow. God wants church growth and growth is good for both church and society.

In four brief years, 1973 to 1977, the worldwide explosion of church growth thinking was greatly helped by Gerber's book circulating in astronomical numbers and being used by churches in forty-seven languages. Theological training schools used it. District superintendents used it. Bishops used it. Christian leaders all over the world had been looking for a tool to get pastors and lay leaders of ordinary churches, missionaries, and seminary teachers thinking about church growth opportunities in the light of the growth they had achieved. The Gerber manual *was* that tool. Consequently, as soon as leaders read about it in the *Church Growth Bulletin* and other magazines, or heard about it from missionaries or fellow pastors, they got busy holding church growth workshops and rousing Christians to the church growth challenge.

Four astounding results usually followed:

1. Pastors and churches of all imaginable varieties faced the facts of growth. This was a first-time experience for many of them. They had not been talking about church growth. They had not been praying about it. They were not acutely conscious of it. Then in the course of the church growth workshop they saw the facts.

2. Their conscience was aroused. When they heard the biblical mandate and charted their own record of growth against it, they were pricked in their hearts.

3. They began to estimate the real possibilities of growth. The workshop brought addresses on how other churches in their part of the world were growing, and how to recognize receptive pieces of the population mosaic. They heard about the great role laymen play in church growth and the way to acquire church growth eyes. They began to talk to one another about the possibilities in their particular situation, their city, their denomination. They began to pray for church growth. God opened their eyes and they saw the real opportunities for growth. Pessimism declined and they began to count on God's resources.

4. Wholly beyond the directions and expectations of Dr. Gerber and his helpers, men who passed through his seminar on church growth launched many probes, tried many new experiments in church growth, and answered many Macedonian calls.

71

What does the amazing story of global goal setting mean to mainline church leaders in the United States? I suggest that you rejoice in it, adapt it, and use it. Expose your church to the five-step process that follows, and use the Gerber manual or write one of your own.

Step 1. When the group gathers, first of all lay a firm biblical base. Present church growth as something that Christ commands and that men and women, boys and girls need desperately. Finding Christ and becoming part of his Body is what church growth essentially is. Being in Christ satisfies the deepest hunger of the human heart. It assuages spiritual thirst. Present church growth, then, as a mandate from God. Base it firmly on the Bible. God wants his lost children found.

Step 2. Let those attending the meeting, whether the laity of one congregation or the pastors of one district, chart their past growth. They should see clearly the patterns of past growth. They should spend considerable time working their way through the annual records of their own membership. Let them analyze past growth and discuss its various strands. Help them see what factors caused growth and what, alas, caused stagnation. Chart and discuss biological growth, transfer growth, conversion growth, losses to the world, removals, average worship attendance, and average Sunday school attendance over the past decade. In the era just before us, Christians ought to be able to talk about evangelism and church growth with the same ease they now talk about the World Series, juvenile delinquency, and the sexual revolution. Give them much practice in talking and praying about church growth.

Step 3. Saturate participants with population facts about their neighborhood, city, or countryside. Make sure they see the enormous unchurched populations about them. It is common for Christians to think America is fairly well churched. A few communities may be. In some places middle-class Americans are well churched; but when we think of the population as a whole, particularly city populations, we must think of enormous numbers of shepherdless, masterless materialists.

Step 4. Help them see that in these populations substantial church growth is not only possible, but may be actually going on. Whenever Christians do what wins people to Christ and leads them into baptized membership in his Church, churches grow. Most nongrowth is due to the fact that church people are spending their time, talents, and money doing good things that do *not* find and fold lost sheep. It is as simple as that. Church growth is abundantly possible if church leaders will recruit and train as many class-two leaders as it does class-one leaders. The current popular concept that the growth of the church in modern indifferent America is impossible must be shown to be erroneous and really a bit ridiculous. Accounts of churches which are growing ought to become part of the furniture of the mind of Baptists, Presbyterians, United Methodists, and Episcopalians all across the United States.

Step 5. Finally, in an atmosphere of true faith and prayer, let participants project the growth they believe God wants to give them. When they put that projection on the chart next to their own past record, they can expect new insight and determination to be born. Goal setting is a rewarding activity in ordinary churches.

The Objective Is Church Growth

Our objective must be very clear. We are *training the laity to make churches grow.* Do not phrase your objectives in vague generalities and diversionary platitudes.

The Church has many duties, and we train persons to carry them out. Let me, therefore, at the outset, say that we are training lay Christians to find and fold lost sheep. We are not training them to go out and beat the bushes, or to conduct a token search, or to tell the story, or to name the

Name, the most recent blessed vagueness to come out of Geneva. One may have to beat the bushes as he searches for lost sheep, but the aim is never just to beat the bushes. We do certainly tell the story, but the aim is never merely to tell the story.

We must be especially careful not to substitute training men and women to do other things for training them to make the church grow. There are many other good things. We want quality Christians. We want biblically literate Christians. The prayer life of the laity can usually be improved. In this world of many different denominations, Christian unity and cooperation do not come automatically. We must train lay Christians to regard their Church as only a part of the whole. "Joint Action for Mission" is a useful slogan.

I repeat, these are all good things to do. But none of them must be substituted for puposeful, costly, continued evangelism, which adds members to the church and multiplies new churches throughout the population.

A Lincoln story aptly illustrates the point. I am a teetotaller and a prohibitionist, but I still like the story. During the first two years of the Civil War, the North had been losing battles. Lincoln would appoint a general, and promptly he would lead his army to defeat. Morale was low. Lincoln was desperate. Then in the West, Grant started winning battles and gaining territory. At just that point a deputation of Christian women waited on Lincoln. "Mr. President," they said, "we have come to beg you to remove General Grant. He drinks whiskey all the time and is often drunk. He sets a very bad example to our boys. He is unworthy to be at the head of our armies." Lincoln leaned across the table and asked softly, "Ladies, can you tell me what brand of whiskey he drinks?" None of them knew. "I wish you could tell me," Lincoln went on, "because I would send a keg of that whiskey to every one of my generals."

Lincoln had high goals to free the slaves and to preserve

the union, but he saw clearly that unless victories were won, none of these other goals would be achieved. In training the laity, we must have a similar clarity of vision.

The goal that we must place steadily before us is to train men and women, boys and girls to evangelize so that people *do* believe on Jesus Christ, *are* baptized, do *become* responsible members of his Church, *do go out* to win others to Christ, and *do multiply* cells of the redeemed units of peace and righteousness. Our training scheme must intend to achieve all five of these ends. Leading people to believe on Jesus Christ is a temporary goal unless they become members of his Body and remain in an obedient relationship to the Head.

Our churches are suffering from decades of deceitful consolation for evangelistic failure. You know the process. So do I. We have all engaged in it. We have a season of refreshing, an evangelistic campaign, a special speaker, or a calling caravan—names are legion. After it is all over, we trot out the words that console us. The event resulted in a "marked sense of unity." "The members never felt closer." "We were drawn back to our initial commitment to Jesus Christ." "We revealed in ministry the love of God for all who suffer." "We have a heightened sense of the presence of God's Holy Spirit."

These consoling words are, of course, true, but they conceal the fact that few prodigals have walked back across the threshold of their Father's House. The training program of which I speak must consciously and resolutely turn away from all these deceptive phrases, all these rationalizations of defeat.

We must intend objective numerical church growth and be honest enough, if we do not get it, to say so. We must not let fear of failure permit us the luxury of defining our goals so that we cannot fail. Many evangelistic campaigns are from the start doomed because those who plan them also plan that the measure of success will not be the number found. It is as if the shepherds going out to search for lost

75

sheep met at the gate to announce that it would make no difference how many were found.

In contradistinction to all this defensive strategy, let us plainly train men and women, boys and girls to find lost sheep and to keep careful count of those they successfully bring back to the fold. Fishers of fish count only those above the legal limit. The others they throw back. Fishers of men ought to count only those who are successfully grafted into the Body.

In 1800, Methodist class meetings did not just happen while Coke, Asbury, and others were aiming at a dozen other good outcomes. Methodist laymen were incorporated into class meetings and were trained to go out and establish others. That was the bull's eye. Let us train the laity to shoot at the bull's eye.

Let us train lay Christians to measure church growth. This aspect of our task will be congenial to most of our members. Americans are accustomed to exact goals. Yale University has just raised an endowment fund of 370 million dollars. Not some millions, not a couple of dozen millions, but 370 million dollars. Businessmen try to make their investments pay 9 percent. The American Gross National Product, GNP, rises at 6 percent per annum. Since inflation gallops along at about 7 percent per annum, most institutions try to raise salaries at 10 percent per annum. A school superintendent can tell you the growth index of Spanish-American children in his school system and how many of them he expects to have in 1990.

Some lay Christians use statistical representation of growth and decline routinely in their businesses. They would be delighted to employ their know-how in the church field. They could chart the growth rates of several different strands in your membership—the retired, the senior leaders of the community, the young adults, the youth, the children. They could teach the others so that your task force maintained a clear idea of what the actual situation was.

In training the laity as we press such considerations, are we in danger of becoming mechanical, of running ahead of the Holy Spirit, of submitting to the tyranny of statistics? Are we engaging in numerolatry? Definitely not. We are simply keeping track of the number of the redeemed and the growth rate of those filled with the Holy Spirit. We are observing accurately which methods God is blessing to the growth of his Household and which he is not. The physician is not tyrannized by statistics when he takes your blood pressure. Neither is the minister when he charts carefully the growth rate of his congregation.

Past records of growth and decline are important, but even more important are projections of growth. As we shall see presently, this is an important part of the measuring process.

Give Class-Two Workers Field Experience

In mobilizing the laity for the propagation of the faith and training the task force for church growth, field practice is essential.

The minister properly expounds the scriptures that require evangelism and have made the Church an evangelizing Body. He properly exhorts Christians to go out and tell other people of the Savior, to invite them to the Church, to serve and love them into the Kingdom. But if training lay Christians stops with expounding and exhorting, there will be no growth. Too many times under the inspiration of the pulpit, laymen have gone out to evangelize, have made mistakes in presentation or been rudely turned away, and have come back licking their wounds and vowing never to evangelize again. Exhortation must be followed by field training. Internship is a necessary part of training.

In a similar way, the study of a book on church growth by a group of Christians is an excellent thing to do. It gets the task force one step closer to effectiveness. But no matter how good the book, you cannot learn to play tennis by reading a book. Practice is required. The eye and the muscles must be trained. Errors must be made and corrected; there is no other way. Proclaiming Jesus Christ as God and Savior and persuading men to become members of his Church is an exceedingly complex process. It is carried on at different levels. Presentations cannot be canned, because every individual to whom we speak is different and requires a different approach.

Here is one place where measurements give rich rewards. When you measure the outcome in terms of reliable members of ongoing churches you know what kinds of training to emphasize and what not to emphasize. Much evangelism operates in the midst of perpetual fog. It does the right thing. It says the right words. But it never measures the outcome, and it lives in blissful ignorance of what has really happened. Judicious use of feedback based on accurate measurement brings laypersons and pastors out of the fog into the sunlight. They can see for miles. They discern at once what the strategy in the next year should be.

Each denomination, each conference, each synod or diocese, each region, and, to a limited extent, each congregation needs, therefore, to institute purposeful research in church growth. That will throw a flood of light on what ought to be done now and in the years ahead. Fortunately, America is blessed with large numbers of sociologists who have analyzed our society from thousands of points of view. Church growth research can harness these sociological findings to the purposes of God. Denominations and congregations can set their goals in the light of the real situation.

For example, the years ahead are going to bring an enormous influx of Mexican-Americans to the United States. *No* denomination at present is planning to transform *millions* of these fine people into devout practicing

Christians, who are consciously a part of the Body of Christ and intend to obey his commands. Purposeful research into the whole Mexican-American scene and intelligent feedback into the local and denominational plans for action would enable any denomination to do more than the pitifully little they now do in this field. Part of the problem is, of course, that the size of the Spanish-speaking community has increased tremendously. Churches do not see the enormous opportunity. What does it mean that at least six million and perhaps ten million undocumented immigrants from Mexico are now in the United States? What does it mean to a powerful Church marching under Christ's Command to seek and save the lost?

So, Train the Laity

All three terms in the title of this chapter are crucially important:

1. *For Church Growth*. The training must be *for church growth*. The goal must be crystal clear. It must be defended against multitudinous good things which obscure it.

2. *The Laity*. The laity must be trained. The process may start with minister and employed staff. But only as it surges out beyond these and enrolls great numbers of your members will the danger you are in be averted. Your goal should be clear, a specified number of women and men, girls and boys, old and young, rich and poor, black and white, out evangelizing every week.

3. *Training*. The process we are setting forth is education or *training*. It includes motivating, goal setting, instructing, exhorting, building up convictions, and harnessing sociological data of all sorts. It also must include much practice and continual improvement in the light of feedback. Church growth is not some quick and easy gimmick. We are not saying, "Use these words. Push these buttons. Pray these prayers, and presto your church will grow." That is what

we are *not* saying. Rather, we are advocating a costly Christian life, an unalterable purpose to seek and save the lost, convictions deeply aligned with Scripture, a high view of the Church, and a training system to pass these on to millions of workaday Christians. I give you *training the laity for church growth*. A most rewarding and challenging task.

V

Helping the
"Small Church" Grow

In the Beginning . . .

The "small church" is the oldest local structure of the Christian movement. When the apostle Paul was writing his Epistles to the church at Corinth, Rome, or some other city, he was not writing to one large congregation that met in a large parish church or a cathedral with a steeple. He was writing, in each case, to a federation of several or more small congregations that, together, made up the Church of that city.

Each of the city's several congregations met in a *home*.[1] Synagogues, marketplaces, and other public settings were not usually a congregation's meeting place. Homes were the norm. Usually they were the larger homes of persons of some means, and sometimes homes were expanded to accommodate a growing congregation. But they did meet in homes, and the Christian movement greatly expanded in the first three centuries through the structure of small congregations meeting in homes.

That early church growth was undoubtedly based on a series of strategies something like the following: (1) the arriving missionary in a new city would prioritize the winning of some relatively affluent person whose home could be used as a meeting place for a new congregation; (2) that house church would grow to the limits of its facilities, occasionally expanding those facilities to permit more growth; (3) that congregation would assist the missionary in the starting of other small churches in the city. It was especially through the proliferation of these small congregations that the Christian movement won perhaps a majority of the citizens of the Roman Empire. The *small church* enabled the earliest period of very great church growth.

In the twentieth century, the small church is still the most prevalent expression of congregational structure. In some countries and cultures congregations still meet in homes, but in other countries and cultures, congregations meet in small chapels or other special buildings. And, in many places on the globe, these small churches are once again enablng a period of very great expansion for the Christian Church.

But in America, where there are also many small churches, it is widely assumed that small churches are a deterrent to contagious Christian movement, that "small churches cannot grow." This assumption is inconsistent with the apostolic Church's experience as well as much contemporary experience and warrants examination. We contend that with an adequate faith, self-understanding, and strategy, *American* small churches *can* be the agents of very significant Christian evangelism and church growth.

What Is "Small"?

Many church leaders *think* of their church as "small" when objective standards would not support that designation. It *is* important to distinguish between small and not-small churches because if members of a small church think their church is smaller than it really is, their false perception strongly influences their self-esteem, dreaming, and planning. We dream and plan on the basis of *our perceptions* of the facts rather than upon reality. So, when members of a middle-sized church erroneously perceive their church as small, this scripts them for small-church achievements. Unfortunately, most local church leaders think of their church as smaller than it is. For instance, in comparison with the other three hundred thousand Protestant congregations of America, would you estimate your church to be in the smallest third, the middle third, or the largest third?

Two standards will help you determine the accuracy of your estimate: membership and worship attendance. In confirmed membership, the smallest third have 100 or fewer members, the middle third have between 100 and 225 members, and those churches with over 225 members constitute the largest third of all American Protestant congregations. In worship attendance, the smallest third have forty-five or fewer people on an average Sunday, the churches in the middle range have from 45 to 120 in worship, and the "largest" churches are those with more than 120 in average worship attendance.[2]

But the *social structure* of your congregation is a more important factor than mere numbers, although the two factors are related. We are suggesting that a church that is essentially a *single cell*, in which virtually all the members regularly interact with almost all the others, is rightly designated a "small" church. *Multicell* churches, where a given member interacts with some members all the time, but with others only occasionally or rarely, are not by this definition small churches.

The very significant difference between single-cell and multicell churches is suggested by Dr. Ray Sells' distinction between the "Winnebago" church and the "Volkswagen" church. The small church

is like a Winnebago. It is one fellowship, one family, and everyone who belongs, belongs to one another and to the full

83

life of the church, and all ride together. There are no strangers aboard, and when one goes they all go along. . . . The single-cell (Winnebago) is a contained, intimate, sharing fellowship with everyone a full partner in the journey and the fellowship.[3]

But Sells, extending the analogy, explains that

in the larger membership multicell church there are too many to load aboard one Winnebago, so there are smaller groups, fellowship and program opportunities which serve as the vehicle of fellowship and belonging. There are many Volks- wagens for the many small and diverse groups in a multicelled church. Each smaller unit, group or class provides room and space for its members and no more, and these groups, like Volkswagens on the highway, may pass one another and persons may wave, but they feel no compelling reason to know every person in every group. . . . In a multicell (Volkswagen) church there are a variety of Volkswagens, each self-contained with a smaller single-cell fellowship which functions like the single-cell church. It is a group where fellowship and belonging are experienced, and the vehicle for making one's way through the life of the congregation.

So, the important criterion is the church's social structure, involving the interpersonal communication patter of the membership. To summarize (and extend) what has been said: a *small* church is a single-cell (although admittedly, many single-cells are "stretched" to a larger size than one would logically expect). A *middle-sized* church is a multicell congregation. And a *large church* is a multicongregational church. More on that later.

The above distinctions enable us to see that the small church is a special type of church, not merely a miniature version of a large church. Lyle E. Schaller delineates the distinction in a way that shows the futility of trying to merge several small churches to make one big church. Schaller portrays the large church as analogous to a pumpkin and the small church as analogous to a squash.

Schaller explains that a squash is of the same *family* as a pumpkin, but it is *not* the same thing. It is a different specie of the same family. There are important differences. For instance, a squash church can get along without a "pastor," but a pumpkin church cannot. The squash church people do much of the caring ministry; all they need is a "preacher." Squashes are much more durable, and tougher, than pumpkins. You can hardly kill a small squash church, and some pastors (and church bureaucrats) have tried. And because a squash and a pumpkin are not the same, we must treat them differently. You simply cannot put, say, five squashes together and expect to create a pumpkin.

Now, it should *not* be thought that all small single-cell churches are pretty much the same and have no affinities with multicell and multicongregational churches. Knowledge of a church's size and its social structure is not all the information needed, and may not accurately indicate that church's style, emphasis, alliances, problems, strengths, or potential. For instance, a small Mennonite church will probably have more things in common with a large Mennonite church than with a small Lutheran church. Or a small church serving blue-collar-worker families may have more things in common with a large church serving the same population than with a small church serving primarily retired professional people. So size and social structure are not the only ways to categorize or analyze a local church. But they are increasingly productive.

A good literature, long needed, is now emerging on the small single-cell church. A collection entitled *Small Churches Are Beautiful* represents a spectrum of focused practical scholarship in behalf of the small church.[4] Carl S. Dudley's *Making the Small Church Effective* is must reading for all leaders of small churches, lay and clergy.

Dudley loves the small church, knows it as well as any American scholar, and believes it to have a characteristic strength, even a genius. That genius is the network of personal, caring relationships that is the essence of a Christian congregation. The small church is a single-caring cell that embraces every member of the congregation. In such a cell, each member knows, or knows about, all the other members on a regular basis. The active members of small churches typically *love* their churches and experience a very deep sense of belonging. Dudley observes that "belonging to the church is like being a member of the family."

About half the Protestant congregations of North America are small churches in the sense we have defined them. They are the original form the church took, they are widespread today, they are strong and tough, they are loved by their people. But can they grow in America's cultural soils? In what ways is the Great Commission viable for single-cell churches? What can small-church leaders reasonably expect, pray, and plan for? Eight propositions summarize much of what is presently known about small-church growth.

How They Grow

1. *The small church usually grows with difficulty.*

Small churches experience difficulty in outreach and expansion, but not for the causes usually offered—no growth potential in the community and/or lack of vision in the church's leadership. Occasional situations, where most of the people have moved out and those remaining are already churched, do exist in isolated instances.[5] But such circumstances do not exist nearly as frequently as local church leaders believe. In many communities where no-growth-potential was long assumed, a new church has come in with a different style or an aggressive outreach to previously neglected people and has grown in the very soil where such growth was *assumed* to be impossible. Robert Schuller is near the objective truth when he exclaims, in the film *How to Grow a Church,* that "the church can grow anywhere except Death Valley or the North Pole. You've got to have people, but if there are people around the church, then any church can grow!"

And it is also true that some congregational leadership lacks the Great Commission vision and will that can enable church growth. But clear and faithful preaching and teaching, combined with sharing the facts about the church and the community, can frequently awaken the vision and will.[6] Those of us who consult with congregations are increasingly impressed with what local church leaders are capable of doing in church growth planning and outreach when we identify with them, get their attention, share and teach the necessary facts, and encourage them.

Carl S. Dudley exposes the *real* reason why small churches grow with difficulty. "A small church cannot grow in membership without giving up something very precious: the basic satisfaction that everyone knows, or knows about, everyone else."[7] That is, a small single-cell church cannot grow *very* significantly and *remain* a small single-cell church in which everyone knows everyone else, and belonging is like being in a *family.* This is precisely the kind of church most members of small churches deeply prefer. The prospects of growth threaten the very nature of the small church and the satisfaction that the members experience. The people in some small churches feel already stretched to the relational limits. They sense that if they grow, they will lose contact with many of the church's members.

The small church will not experience new growth unless the members face this anxiety head on and work through it. Once they do face and work through it, they may then be emotionally free to consider new evangelism.

2. *The small church has already grown more than it "should have."*

Let us not sell short the growth potential of the small church. In most cases it has already grown, adding new members who were really attracted to it, and the original members welcomed and assimilated them.

Not only has the usual small church grown numerically in the past, it has grown structurally as well. That is, it began as a single-cell congregation in which everyone interacted with everyone else regularly and evolved in a larger stretched-cell congregation in which everyone now interacts or hears about everyone else on a regular basis. If Mrs. Crenshaw's college son is bringing a girl home for Christmas, in a single-cell congregation Mrs. Torres would hear about it from Mrs. Crenshaw, but in a stretched-cell congregation she might hear the news from Mrs. Boyer, but hear about it she would.

It is still one social cell, but it has been stretched by additional members to a point where it is difficult to grow more and still remain a kind of unitary social cell. This brings on the anxiety about more growth that Dudley refers to. Members of this stretched-cell structure understandably are anxious about still more growth. The congregation's growth usually levels off here. It is from this point that more growth is difficult.

But it is useful to perceive and to remind the members that church growth has already taken place in their past, presumably in part because they have strengths and attractive qualities as a congregation. Indeed, their quiet but contagious strength is indicated by the fact that they have already grown to a greater size than any secular primary group type of organization in the community.

3. *The small church can easily replace existing members.*

Gradually, as members die off or move away, the stretched-cell congregation can rather easily replace them by assimilating new members into its ranks. Replacement is especially possible during the first two or three seasons after, say, a family moves away. For that period of time, the previous size of the stretched-cell structure is felt to be normal and the people feel a vacancy within their ranks.

That feeling can subside after two or three seasons, and the new contracted size is then felt to be normal. So it is important for church leaders to move for replacement outreach as quickly as possible.

The congregation can rather easily assimilate new people up to the size they are used to being. These new members typically come from people already on the fringes of the church or from among the pool of friends, relatives, neighbors, and fellow workers already linked to at least some of the congregation's members. Many churches engage in this replacement outreach rather naturally and spontaneously, which is why many such churches have been approximately the same size for many years, and in some cases for decades.

4. *The small church can grow slowly but surely by "adopting" new members.*

Carl S. Dudley emphasizes that, because the single-cell church functions like an extended family, the most natural ways for this family to grow are family style. One of these ways is by *birth,* but many of the church's children eventually move away. The other way is by the adoption of new people into the family, and this is a method for relatively slow small-church growth.[8]

Adoption not only includes the development of an appropriate relationship between the new member and each of the other members, but also involves the intentional introduction of the new member into the story of the congregation—its history, traditions, victories, and secrets. It takes time for the new member to join and absorb the history of that church so that it becomes part of his or her story too. Because of the time involved, few small churches could adopt more than six to eight family units per year.

Dudley points out that the small congregation most typically adopts new members during a time of crisis or transition in the person's life. The congregation reaches and assimilates these persons by doing what the small congregation does best, caring ministry to persons.

5. *The small church can grow greatly by multiplying the cells within its ranks.*

I am sure that John Wimber, of the Fuller Evangelistic Association, is right in contending that if the small church is to experience great contagious growth, "You must help them to perceive that a multiple cell church can be healthy." The people in a stretched-cell congregation enjoy the one cell in which everyone knows everyone and they highly value that experience. But with help they can perceive the limits to outreach that the single-cell structure imposes. The leader's great opportunity is to help the people perceive that if they go multicell, each believer can still be meaningfully related to as many people as in a single-cell congregation, and that, for the most part, the long-standing members will still relate to one another. By restructuring their church two or more cells, to go from one Winnebago to several Volkswagens, members of the single-cell church can have the added satisfaction of obeying Christ's Great Commission and sharing what they have to offer to many people who need it.

But *how* this multiplying of cells is done is currently open to some conjecture and dispute. Carl S. Dudley advocates a policy analogous to cellular division. "Like cells of the human body, the church body has *grown by division* of large cells into two or more smaller cells."[9] Thus, in his model, church growth is structurally enabled by the continual division of existing cells in two or more cells, each of which will have room to grow.

I champion the basic strategy of the multiplication of cells, but I doubt that it can usually be done best by cellular division. I know of exceedingly few cases where that has happened, except as a result of a "shootout" where one group leaves in anger and starts another, or where it was the contract and understanding of the cell members all along that they would one day divide. For most existing single-cell churches, and for long-existing cells within larger churches, it would be inordinately painful for them to break up their family-like group, and they would likely resist this policy.[10] Remember, a long-term strategy by this policy would be asking these clanlike church people to divide and experience grief several times. That is an exceedingly difficult policy to implement among people who love and depend on a small single-cell church.

Even if you did succeed in dividing their one cell in two, and later those two into four, you would still discover some unanticipated difficulties in attracting and keeping new people. Why? Because each "new" cell is not really a *new* cell at all, but a colony of an old cell, already having a history, established agenda, tradition, ways of doing things. True, it is easier for a smaller cell-from-division to grow, because there is now felt room for growth within each cell. But new members would still feel like homesteaders, trying to break in and be accepted on the turf of the pioneers who came before and who have already written the first chapters of the local history. The assimilation of new people into such cells *is* more possible than before, but by conscious slow adoption rather than "spontaneous expansion."

The way to enable very significant church growth is by multiplying units, not through cellular division, but through *cellular reproduction*. This distinction is not mere semantics. This strategy advocates the creation of essentially new cells as ports of entry for undiscipled people. This strategy does not divide old cells, but leaves them intact. For instance, one or more key members of the old cell help start a new cell for outreach. They "fertilize" the new cell, and after several months of recruiting members for it, they return to their former cell involvement and/or move out to help start still another new cell. The recruited new members become a cell with new leaders.

Several arguments seem to commend this cellular-reproduction approach to the multiplying of cells for outreach. This model is supported by many actual parish cases with which I am familiar. It is a more possible model to implement, for it eliminates the grief that the other model inflicts. The new cells, so created, really are new with a new agenda and history to begin for new people. This approach will provide more adequately for the assimilation of new people, for their involvement in setting the group's goals and writing its agenda, and for their feelings of real belonging and ownership.

In summary, the small church can grow by undergoing the kinds of structural changes that enable its potential growth to take place. Eventually, the growth history of a once small church into a large church is experienced by four major structural changes: (1) it begins as a single-cell church, in which everyone knows and regularly interacts with everyone else; (2) it grows into a stretched-cell in which, now, everyone interacts or hears about everyone regularly; (3) then, by decision and planning (it doesn't casually happen), they become a multicell congregation, coordinating several or more primary groups whose members interact with one another and who may or may not interact with a given person in another group; (4) eventually, the growing church becomes a multicongregational church, and this permits its very substantial growth. Such a structure provides two, three, or more worshiping congregations, meeting for worship at various times, perhaps in various settings, styles, and even languages. This structure also permits the evolution of a number of other *large groups* that function to some degree as a congregation, as for example, a church men's club, which has its own meeting, devotional and singing, elected leaders, treasury, programs and projects, and membership roll. In this multicongregational structure, which includes both worshiping congregations and large groups, *each* congregation may have two or more cells within it. The church then looks something like a federation of multicell congregations.

6. *The small church can grow by the Bridges of God.*

Small-church members are not, by and large, socially aggressive people. Many of them are good hosts and hostesses, very warm toward visitors in their homes and churches. But they do not generally function aggressively on other people's turf. This personality trait is one reason why they find special meaning in the small church.

This personality trait causes them to balk at the thought of their church becoming more "evangelistic." They balk because they equate evangelism with visiting strangers on their turf, verbalizing the Gospel and eliciting a response in one transaction, and then assimilating these responding strangers into their single-cell church. They know they "ought" to so evangelize, but they defer acting because they find it monumentally difficult to engage strangers. Besides, to welcome strangers into membership would undermine their type of church as a fellowship where virtually everyone knows everyone else well.

But, the perspective that comes from church growth research reveals that outreach to strangers is not necessary for a church to grow. Indeed, that is not typically the way the church grows significantly in any culture on earth. Always, when the church is growing most contagiously, its members are reaching people, relatives, friends, neighbors, and fellow workers within their social web, as we have delineated earlier in this book.[11]

It is not reasonable to expect most small-church members to engage strangers, but they can engage undiscipled persons within their web of social contacts. Indeed, this is how their church usually grows by replacement and adoption. What the church sometimes does naturally and spontaneously must now be done intentionally and programmatically in every season of the church's year.

Such a strategy would involve the identifying of undiscipled persons from among the relatives and friends of the church's active credible Christians. Make lists of such persons already linked to people in the church. Keep files on them. Visit them every season. When you visit them at a time when they seem to be receptive, invite them to come to church and to explore the faith. *Especially* identify and reach out to undiscipled friends, relatives, neighbors, and fellow workers of your new Christians. They have more existing bridges to more undiscipled persons than your old members do, and, moreover, the persons within the social webs of new Christians are more likely to be receptive than most other groups in the community.

It is possible for a small congregation to reach out within the social networks of its members and experience significant growth without experiencing significant loss of their sense of unified fellowship. This is the heart of the way forward for small congregations that want to be faithful to Christ's outreach mandate. The bridges-of-God principle can operate as a much greater strategy than most small-church leaders have perceived. And it can be the church's ongoing strategy. It never becomes outmoded; you never have to look for a "newer" strategy. As long as human nature remains consistent, undiscipled people will be most responsive to credible Christians who are already within their social network. As long as the church is winning new people, their friends, relatives, and co-workers will continually provide new population pools for outreach.

The United Methodist Church of Bruce, Mississippi, discovered the viability and power of this principle. That church, in a community of some two thousand people, had been plateaued at about 175 members for many years. In 1977, it received only four new members by profession of faith, and experienced a net increase from 174 to 175 members.

In January, 1978, Pastor Ben Goodwin attended a Conference on Church Growth led by these two writers. He caught on to the bridges-of-God principle and began imagining what that would look like in his community. He met with his lay leaders and shared what he had learned. They surveyed their town and found about 240 persons not involved in anyone's church. They discovered that virtually all these 240 persons were linked already to one or more church members by work, friendship, neighborhood, or kin. They gave these members six weeks of training and sent them out to invite the undiscipled people to follow Christ or to explore this Way in the church. In the next four and one-half months they received fifty-four new members, forty-six of them by profession of faith. The church is still growing powerfully as the church continues to walk across the bridges that God has provided in existing social networks. Goodwin reports that now his people "believe that they can do anything." Thousands of small congregations can, and will, reap that same kind of harvest.

7. *The small church can continue to grow as the pastor changes from a "shepherd" to a "rancher."*

Naturally, the role and leadership of the pastor are crucial variables in the growth of a church at every stage in the process.[12] His or her role becomes especially crucial when the growing church has created about as many groups as one pastor can adequately shepherd. Despite the fact that the shepherd role of the clergy is the historically dominant image, Lyle E. Schaller contends that for further church growth to be possible, the pastor will have to become a rancher. Schaller's important distinction is worth rehearsal: The rancher

> *manages* the ranch and *delegates* to various helpers, such as the foreman, cowboys and others, the responsibility for the *direct* care of the various herds of cattle scattered across the range of the horses, and of whatever other livestock may be on the ranch. Ranchers are very much *concerned* about the welfare of

95

every animal on the premises, but their basic responsibility is to manage the total situation, not to be directly involved with the care of every animal.[13]

Schaller would point out that the good rancher-pastor does not get out of the ministry by becoming *only* a manager of ministry. Such a pastor is involved in actual shepherding ministry for those who work with him/her, modeling for them the shepherding role. But the rancher knows that he/she cannot do all the shepherding because there are now too many herds and animals on the ranch for one person to do all the shepherding. So the rancher, while doing some actual shepherding, now manages the shepherding of the several (or more) people who now do most of the direct shepherding. Schaller's key point regarding sustained congregational growth stresses the greater growth potential of the rancher role of ministry.

The rancher feels good when the herds increase in number and the total of the cattle doubles. By contrast the shepherd feels frustrated when the number of sheep increases to the point that they naturally tend to divide into two or three flocks. He can be with only one flock at a time! There is an obvious limit to the number of sheep one shepherd can tend in one flock.[14]

8. *Growth committed small churches support new church extension.*

Some small churches will never grow beyond the stretched-cell stage with about seventy-five (or less) in average worship attendance, because some churches are placed in areas of declining population, in which few of the people who remain are unchurched. And some congregations are clan-bound congregations, in a culture or subculture where the clan-bound church is a culturally appropriate form for the church to take. Consequently these are not churches that people of other clans would want to join. Indeed, for many reasons it can be said that "not every squash ought to grow up to be a pumpkin" (Schaller).

Such small congregations are not thereby excused from the Great Commission. They too are called to help reach the people who are too far away (geographically, culturally, or linguistically) for their church to reach them. The plan in this case is to zealously support the extension growth of Christ's Church through a strategy of new church planting.[15]

Fresh support of new church extension is one way to get thousands of small churches involved in outreach mission. And it is one place to begin with churches that do have growth opportunity but do not desire growth.

For instance, my colleague Mr. Vance Archer reports the following intriguing case study. In a section of metropolitan Nashville, Tennessee, two congregations each decided that they were "almost big enough," and each set a limit on future growth, so as to "remain a family." To their credit, however, they saw a large reachable population, and the two congregations helped sponsor, promote, staff, and guide the first years of a new congregation. Both sponsoring churches became very involved, from helping select the site, to helping build the first unit, to helping call on the first prospects.

Indeed, these two churches got *too* involved. Their involvement with the new church gave them what Dr. McGavran calls "church growth eyes." They began to look afresh at their own immediate mission fields, decided that their family enjoyment was secondary to Christ's mission, set new growth goals, and began reaching out again. In the last several years, one church has increased 50 percent, the other by 100 percent. And the new church is growing too.

God has great missionary dreams and plans for small congregations of all denominations in America. As in the first centuries, and as in many parts of the globe today, our small churches will experience new self-esteem, goal setting, planning, outreach, growth, and power. Although we want to know much more, and will, we already know some of the ways forward for the small church.

VI

Reaching People
Through New Congregations

Most mainline North American Protestants do not presently perceive an elementary fact, a fact they must be brought to perceive before contagious Christian movement will take place in North America. A renaissance of new church extension must take place. Thousands of new congregations will be needed for North American Protestantism to fulfill her Great Commission mandate.

Most North American laypeople and their leaders would not presently advocate this cause, but would perhaps voice the opposite: "Doesn't this continent already have over three hundred thousand congregations? Shouldn't that be enough? Is not our real problem a fierce competition between congregations, of which we already have too many? What we need is not more churches, but better churches, more cooperation, more unity."

But, in spite of what everybody knows, North America needs thousands of new congregations. I believe that when you see the evidence, you will concur and will see that part of your congregation's mission lies in the sponsorship of still more congregations.

What is that evidence? First, new congregations are needed simply because they are much more evangelistically prolific than old congregations, and the Great Commission to "go . . . and make disciples" needs great numbers of people who do that best. Dr. Lyle E. Schaller reports that

> The most important single argument for making new church development a high priority is this is the most effective means for reaching unchurched persons. Numerous studies have shown that 60 to 80 percent of the new adult members of new congregations are persons who were not actively involved in the life of any worshipping congregation immediately prior to joining that new mission. By contrast, most long established churches draw the majority of their new adult members from persons who transfer in from other congregations. New Christians as well as young adults born since 1940 are found in disproportionately larger numbers in new missions than in the older churches.[1]

The second argument comes from the sheer massive mobility of our own people, those already won to the faith and active in our present churches. Schooling, marriage, employment opportunities, and a host of other factors cause our people to relocate their place of residence. Increasing numbers of them are moving to places that do not have a congregation of their denomination or tradition. Some communities or sections of communities are virtually bereft of churches compared to the opportunity. If our mobile people were once worth winning, they are now worth keeping, by following the population mobility patterns with aggressive new church planting.

These two arguments by themselves are enough to pull us toward a new era of the "planned parenthood" of churches, "planned parenthood" in the earlier (Genesis 1:27-28) sense of multiplying and filling the earth, rather than the more recent sense of limiting population. The North American Church needs to get off the pill and start propagating the family of churches once again.

We all recognize, of course, that some small communities are overchurched. Arthur County, Nebraska, for instance, has a total of six hundred souls and nine churches. Other examples can readily be given. However, when we have given the most generous acknowledgment to overchurching and compared it with the situation in most communities, especially large urban communities, we see that the American problem is not overchurching. It is underchurching. Perhaps a third argument will clinch this conviction in your mind.

Sheer Numbers Prove that America Must Have Thousands of New Churches

The huge unchurched populations demand millions more Christians. For these we shall need all the present churches and thousands of new churches.

Enormous numbers of North Americans are either totally without church connection or, while their names are on some roll somewhere, are not active disciples. Remember that the 1980 population of the United States hovers at 225 million people. To see the situation as it is, the facts call us to divide this 225 million into three great groups.

Group A contains ardent responsible practicing Christians and numbers about sixty million.

Group B contains nominal marginal Christians and numbers about 110 million.

Group C contains about fifty-five million who do not claim to be Christians and are, in fact, materialists, hedonists, humanists, Marxists, and secularists. Millions choose to live like car-driving animals.

Let us concentrate for a moment on Group B, the 110 million nominally religious folk. Enormous numbers may belong to some church or at least register a church preference in surveys, but live from day to day with little consciousness of obedience to a Master. They do not know what being in Christ means. They find it difficult really to believe in God, the forgiveness of sin, or eternal life. They are following no Shepherd and obeying no Lord. They may

101

claim the name Christian, but know nothing of Christ's power. They were baptized, of course, years ago. "It was what we did in our family, you know." They vaguely remember going to Sunday school as children. They attended church some years ago in New York, or was it Alabama, or California? They believe in God; doesn't everyone? They will want a minister to officiate at their funerals. They feel uneasy about their relationship to God and think they will do something about it—sometime. The tremendous importance of starting new churches has to be seen against the backdrop of these multitudes.

Group C is comprised of perhaps fifty-five million Americans who neither belong to any church nor consider themselves Christians. "My wife goes. I don't," says a neighbor of mine. They are fellow Democrats or Republicans. They live on our streets. They meet us at the symphony or at ball games or in supermarkets. They stay at the same hotels and gather at the same reunions. Most of them are "very nice people" who have quietly rejected Christianity as untenable by modern people. They may send their children to Sunday school, but stay home to read the daily paper and mull over their stock portfolios. They read Camus, Playboy, Bertrand Russell, and Fortune.

Some are classified as secular humanists, some as materialists. Many are de facto hedonists in furious pursuit of pleasure. Many are intent on making money and exercising power. They have no meaningful relationship to Jesus Christ as the Savior or Lord. The tremendous importance of starting new churches has to be seen against the backdrop of about fifty-five million who belong in Group C and do not even claim to be Christian.

The picture is complicated by the fact that some of the practicing Christians, some of the marginal Christians, and some of the non-Christians are ethnics, in all, about sixty million of them. Most of these are not going to be won into WASP congregations. They will have to be won into ethnic congregations, which means new churches in a big way. We shall return to this very important consideration later on, for it represents still another formidable argument for extravagant new church planting.

But, much fog obscures our problem, in the sense that many local church leaders (mis)perceive their community as being much more heavily churched than it really is. Once Dr. Winfield Arn was leading a church growth seminar in Ohio. Before the seminar started, he went to a ministerial luncheon. He was cordially received, but found most of the ministers cool to the seminar. "Look," they said, "we have done a good job. We have been here for more than fifty years. We have enough churches. Our doors are open. We have interesting programs. If anyone wants to come, they know where to find us." Dr. Arn took the challenge. He called every church in the area and found out its seating capacity. He called the Chamber of Commerce and City Planning Board and ascertained the total population of the area. He found that if every church were packed three times on Sunday, *only one-third* of the population would have attended.

A major obstacle keeps some of us from easily seeing the real situation. In a population of say fifty thousand there are already fifty churches. Churches are visible everywhere. All citizens could go to church if they wanted to. Why start more churches to face years of struggle before they grow up? The argument against new churches sounds reasonable, but has a fatal flaw. If each of the fifty churches had four hundred ardent, practicing Christians, together they would have only twenty thousand souls, and there are fifty thousand in that area. Even with fifty churches, the population of fifty thousand has thirty thousand whose relationship to Christ is either marginal or nonexistent. Carry this thought one step further. Instead of a hypothetical community of fifty thousand, let us take an actual one. The United States of America has 225 million souls and three hundred thousand churches, including many rural congregations. If each of *them* had *200 serious Christians*, all together the three hundred thousand churches would have only sixty million active Christians and the United States would still contain 165 million who had no saving involvement in any messianic community.

All these estimates I have been giving you are beset with difficulties. Who is a practicing Christian? Who is a born-again Christian? Who is a marginal Christian? Should a woman whose name is on a church roll a thousand miles away, but who never gives and almost never goes, be listed as a non-Christian, a marginal Christian, or a true Christian? If a person has attended church once in the past month, may he or she be presumed to be an active responsible Christian? These questions can be answered in different ways. But, however we answer them, and this is the point, it is absolutely clear that enormous numbers of men and women have yet to believe in Christ, be reconciled to God, and folded into Christ's flock. Make any calculations you wish, the following fact leaps out at you: *enormous numbers of our brothers and sisters have yet to become responsible Christians*. This fact demands action on a new, large scale—action that will win many persons to existing churches, many other to new churches.

Now, since I am making a serious proposal, I must take into account the difficulties that immediately appear to anyone who knows the situation. Let me present four and deal with each.

Apparent Difficulties Stand in the Way

Difficulty One:
The Denominations Do Not Have the Money Required

"Our church is already doing a great deal, and, while it would be nice to multiply churches, we simply cannot afford even to contemplate the additional millions it would take to add hundreds of new churches." Does that sound familiar? Let me attempt two solutions to this objection.

1. Multiplying churches under today's circumstances is biblically required. Any soundly Christian church ought to make sure that its priorities are biblical and balanced. Every church, every denomination, is engaged in five great thrusts, all in the will of God: (1) the church worships God and adores him; (2) the church cares for the flock; (3) the church does good to all and seeks to make God's will effective in society; (4) the church promotes the unity of the church; (5) the church ceaselessly finds the lost and brings them back to the Father's House. It propagates the Church; it reproduces the Household of God. As denomination leaders gaze on the 165 million in the United States and the 3 billion across the seas who have yet to believe on the Savior, *are they laying sufficient emphasis on the propagation of the Gospel, on calling men from death to life?* Are they taking into account the degree of the actual finding of the lost being achieved by their church? Do the Assemblies of God, who start some 240 congregations per year, have proportionally more resources? Do the Southern Baptists, who now start over seven hundred per year?

2. Christians have the resources, and therefore denominations have access to the needed resources if an apostolic vision of the possibilities can attract the funding. People have the resources because of their historic experience of "redemption and lift."[2]

"Redemption and lift" is a by-product of a people's evangelization and life of discipleship. When people are continually converted, they discover Whose they are and therefore who they are. They discover a new self-esteem, sense of dignity, perception of their future possibilities. They get leadership experience within the Church. They desire education, at least for their children. They become liberated from destructive habits. They become more industrious. As a result of influences like these, they

105

prosper, become a different people, and move up the social scale (hence the term "lift"). This whole process is quite visible by the second or third generation. This is why your people have the funds the mission needs. Objective observations of their homes, clothes, cars, and bank accounts will confirm this.

So, lack of financial ability is not the real difficulty. Our mission is being held back by something more subtle, more attitudinal, not so measurable. We are being held back by Difficulty Two, which is afflicting many denominations and many fine Christian people. Let me describe it.

Difficulty Two:
The Denominational Self-Image

Each denomination has such an image, which tends to limit growth to what can be accomplished within that conception of "who we are." To emphasize the point, I am going to illustrate it from one denomination; but let every reader—Episcopalian, Baptist, Pentecostal, or Presbyterian—insert the name of his or her denomination in the following paragraphs wherever he sees the words "United Methodist." Denominational self-image is a subtle part of the thinking of *all* denominations.

Partly because of the experience of redemption and lift, United Methodists see themselves as respectable people, upper-middle-class, educated, propertied people, solid citizens. Executives who live in comfortable homes are likely to be United Methodists. "We have others, of course, but members of our church are quite prominent in this community." The conclusion of this self-image is that, quite unconsciously, we add a sentence: "United Methodist church growth naturally will take place among this kind of people and should be limited to them."

When United Methodists think about it, they will want to challenge that whole line of thought. The United Methodist

Church began as a church of *all* the people. Methodism gloried that multitudes of common people became its members. It multiplied among the masses, the laboring classes. Many labor leaders born in coal mining communities or factory towns, were Methodists. The United Methodist Church *has been* a church of the people, but like many churches its members have moved up to middle-class, and often upper-class.

Redemption and lift have done their work. These important factors affect Christians everywhere, and while it is a positive experience, it contains some trade-offs that frustrate evangelism as usual. Over two or three generations, *redemption and lift separate Christians from their social roots and seal off whole denominations from the lower classes. When that happens, churches cease to grow.*

No denomination wants to limit itself to that segment of society into which God has, through the generations, lifted its present members. No denomination wants to let this status-dominated self-image stand in the way of its multiplying churches in different sections of the population in every state of the Union. You do not want it; yet unless you launch a new era of church-multiplying evangelism, you will do what you do not want. You will reach few outside of the middle-classes. You will remain sealed off.

Difficulty Three:
Liturgical Style

The third difficulty is our liturgical style which inhibits church growth.

As generation succeeds generation, most denominations settle into cultural forms of worship usually quite appropriate to the people they have become, a dignified procedure for the worship of God. Majestic worship, quiet reverent prayer, tuneful singing, impressive organ music, an aesthetic experience characterizes their worship. Since only

107

a small part of the total community "fits" worship forms like this, mainline denominations slide into assuming that only those who like majestic worship and elevated sermons are eligible for evangelization by them. But is this conclusion one that you will stand by? Would the Galileans have liked your liturgical life-style? Would your sermons have communicated with multitudes of the working classes in the Britain of Bunyan, or Knox, or Wesley, or Marx?

To put the question in a different form, suppose you could win large numbers of the American proletariat to the New Life by evangelizing them in less elevated ways and engaging them in a liturgical style quite different from your present practice, ways that "fit" them culturally. *Would you do it?* Would you cease importing culturally foreign music and worship into settings where those forms are not natural? Worship must be expressed in the "heart language" of the target subculture if its members are really to see it, to appropriate it, and to be involved in it.

I ask the same question of every tradition or denomination. Each has a liturgical style that keeps many out of the fold. This difficulty besets all of us.

Initially we have all moved forward through indigenous worship. For instance, The United Methodist Church brought blessing to millions around the world, partly because it brought people to Christ and enabled them to worship God in ways that seemed natural to them, ways that were a long step removed from the stately worship of the Anglican churches of 1750.

Difficulty Four:
Why NEW Churches?

The fourth difficulty that rushes into our minds as we ponder the need for thousands of new churches is this, Why think of *new* churches? Why not bring those we seek into existing congregations? This thoughtful objection deserves a careful answer.

Let me preface it by saying, of course we ought to bring into existing congregations, existing parishes, as many as we can. Few congregations have won all the winnable in their precincts. By all means let us press ahead with near-neighbor evangelism. Let our existing members reach out to their relatives, friends, and intimates and add them to the Lord in existing churches.[3] The church growth movement lays great emphasis on winning the winnable in our own culture group. This is an obvious opportunity and mandate.

But let us remember that the culture groups of every denomination are only a part of the total North American population. Each denomination fits a few segments of the American people. Each denomination exists and is growing or declining chiefly in certain culture groups. For instance, the Christian Church (Disciples of Christ) has American Indian Christian churches, Japanese Christian churches, Black Christian churches. The Christian Church exists in many culture groups. But while this is true, it is also true that the predominant Disciples segment is the fairly well-to-do, fairly well-educated, middle-class community. This is necessarily so. Disciples are good Christians and God blesses good Christians. They get flocks and herds, and vineyards and fields, and factories and preferred stock.

In each piece of the mosaic, faithful members of churches of all denominations rise to the top, and then cease to attract from the bottom. Redemption and lift cut churches off from huge sections of society. If we are going to evangelize the whole population, we must start new churches in every segment of society, led by lay leaders of that subculture, and preached to by ministers of that subculture. We cannot impose middle-class ministers on mass-class churches and expect church growth.

Millions who live in our communities cannot be won into

existing churches. They are too far away, linguistically, culturally, or geographically. If we won all we can into existing churches, millions would be left outside. These cannot be won into existing churches. *For them we need new churches.*

Of course, we have not exhausted all the difficulties experienced in regard to new church prospects. My colleague in this project, Dr. Hunter, has in his role as a denominational executive for evangelism uncovered his own list, which partly overlaps my own: (1) Someone began whispering in the 1960s that Church Extension was no longer "avant garde," "fashionable," or "where the action is." (2) The denomination, now largely upper-middle class and lower-upper class, has lost contact with the lower-middle and upper-lower classes amongst whom some other movements are now so reproductive. (3) We began (mis)perceiving new church extension as a "cost" rather than as our *wisest investment* in the future, and, unlike some other denominations, allowed ourselves to be intimidated by those upfront costs. (4) We began to see our mission field in terms of geography or political units rather than in terms of people-units or subcultures. Unwittingly we slid into the assumption that one church in each political unit is by definition "enough." (5) Our existing local churches became paranoid about helping new congregations get started, seeing them as a potential threat and preferring to try to win and assimilate all receptive people into the already existing congregations. (6) Our district superintendents, who carry the new church extension portfolio in every district of our church, a cadre with a network of awesome potential, came to feel overworked, and lowered new church planting on their hierarchy of priorities. (7) Many of us "remembered," through our anti-small-church bias, those new church starts of the previous generation that "never made it big," and we determined to avoid *that* "mistake" again. (8) Many judicatories, after years of little new church expansion, now have little competency in this special ministry within their own ranks, and are intimidated by the thought of a new beginning from scratch.

Multitudinous Homogeneous Population Units in American Society Call for Tens of Thousands of New Churches

Two sociological facts rise above the horizon like the Matterhorn. Most Protestant congregations are made up of English-speaking, middle-class people. Sixty million ethnic Americans in hundreds of homogeneous units are not going to become members of these English-speaking congregations, no matter how much evangelizing we do.

In Christian thinking in America, this fact has been insufficiently recognized, if indeed it has been recognized at all. It is assumed that if our churches were simply better churches, warmer churches, more integrated churches, more spirit-filled churches, sixty million people who do not feel at home in them could be and would be won. I wish the assumption were true, but it is not.

For instance, think of the six million French Canadians, many of whom believe there ought to be a separate French-speaking state in Canada. Are large numbers of these likely to find Christ and join English-speaking churches? Positively not. Even if they find Christ they will not join English-speaking churches. But many French Canadians, on finding Christ, would cheerfully come to new French-speaking Baptist churches, Presbyterian churches, Pentecostal churches, led by French Canadians, pastored by French Canadians, and openly advocating at church suppers that French Canada should be a separate country.

Are the hundred thousand Portuguese who live south of Boston likely to find Christ and become members of the English-speaking Congregational and Episcopal churches?

111

Even the church where Phillips Brooks preached? The only possibility of their becoming Christian disciples is for them to be evangelized into congregations that are overwhelmingly Portuguese in culture, language, dress, eating habits, marriage patterns, and all the rest.

America is a multicolored mosaic made up of 23 million Blacks, 25 million Spanish Americans, 7 million Italians, 3 million Poles, and about 3 million Asiatic Americans, plus other groups—a total of more than 60 million. These can be discipled; great sections of them are responsive. These millions *want*, without leaving their ethnic identity, to become functioning Americans.

We must make sure they do not become Americans in secular or pagan patterns. But large numbers of them will not be discipled into WASP mainline congregations. True, small numbers are being won and for this we should thank God; but Protestant denominations must deliberately *and soon* cease to be made up overwhelmingly of just one piece or a few pieces of the American mosaic. Protestant denominations must have many congregations of many different ethnic groups. They must have them soon.

That means new churches, a costly multiplication of new churches in ethnic units and subunits all across this vast country. I was in Vancouver, British Columbia, recently and found there a colony of Indians. Idi Amin had driven them out of Uganda. There they were in Vancouver. They emphasized to me that they were not Indian Indians. They were Ugandan refugees. It would be a mistake to conclude that because they were brown, they were East Indians just like the other East Indians. As I talked to these fine people, I came to feel that they were considerably more responsive to the claims of Christ than most Indians from India. Baptist, Methodist, Presbyterian, or Mennonite congregations of Ugandan refugees are quite possible in Vancouver. We should take into account the subunits in each major ethnic unit in North America.

Perhaps some of you are saying, "Wait a minute. These ethnics are mostly Roman Catholics and we must not try to make them Protestants." We used to say that. I used to say that. But it is really beside the point. If the Roman Catholics (or any other denomination) were making their nominals into practicing Christians the situation would be entirely different. But, with the terrific mobility of this land and with the vast spread of materialism, secularity, and skepticism, the day has passed when our evangelism can be deflected by a prospect who (knowing we are, say, Baptists) says, "Thank you for calling, but I am a Roman Catholic." We must go on to ask, "Yes, but are you *currently involved* in a Christian fellowship?"

The fact that millions of Americans are nominally religious with a vague church preference must not become an excuse for withholding the possibility of active Christian discipling among them. We must, of course, avoid a mean-spirited raiding of other congregations. We all agree to that automatically. But the cooperative spirit, as Robert Schuller so well says, must not deflect us from trying to reconcile to God the tremendous numbers of lost men and women in our ministry areas.

To sum up, the thousands of pieces of the American population mosaic in which are millions of God's children who could be reconciled to him in the Body of Christ is abundant reason for thousands of new churches, especially designed to incorporate our ethnic brothers and sisters. Not new churches in general, but new Arabic churches, new Mandarin-speaking Chinese churches, new churches to fit the hundred thousand Jamaican and Trinidadian blacks who have recently come to the United States, new churches to fit the tens of thousands of recent immigrants from Italy now found in most Canadian cities.

Sheer numbers abundantly prove that we need multitudes of new churches. The multitudes of seriously underchurched pieces of the American mosaic cry aloud for new congregations. Now let us turn our attention to ways of establishing new congregations. We might all see the need and yet be stopped, because establishing new churches is a specialized form of Christian activity, a specialized form of evangelism, and requires a clear model of what we propose.

Ways of Establishing New Congregations

Admittedly, the way forward in evangelization through new churches will include what, in mainline Protestantism, has become the traditional model. That is, the denomination or judicatory will buy a strategic tract of land, and perhaps pay the founding minister's salary, or pay for the first building, or loan the fledgling congregation the funds to get started. But this model must not be our only model for launching new congregations. Other models exist, and are thriving, a good thing in view of the inflating expenses of the now traditional model. Lyle E. Schaller is quite right in pointing out that

> the financial subsidization of new congregations is largely a contemporary white, middle and upper class bureaucratic phenomenon, not an inherent requirement for starting new churches. It was not a major component of St. Paul's strategy for new church development.[4]

Space does not permit us to delineate the myriad of optional models now available, but perhaps a litany of some of the options will be sufficient to show the way forward. Other sources, such as *Strategies for New Churches* by Ezra Earl Jones, *Growing New Churches* by Carl Moorhaus, and *Planting New Churches* by Jack Redford, will adequately inform any church or judicatory church extension committee in addition to the resources available in their denomination.[5] A brief litany of models would include the following:

1. Some congregations are started as outpost Sunday

schools in the neighborhood of the target population. Those that make it and thrive, evolve into congregations with a minimal up-front expense. Early Methodism frequently started new churches this way.

2. An established church sometimes opens up a number of outpost preaching points in Ramada Inns, trailer courts, and other similar places. Those that catch on evolve into strong congregations. This model is widely employed in Latin America.

3. Some churches start a second congregation in the same building. Its worship might be of an alternate liturgical style, as in the case of the Central United Protestant Church in Richland, Washington.

4. Some churches start a second or third or fourth language congregation in the same building, as in the case of Temple Baptist Church of Los Angeles, which has one congregation each of Hispanics, Anglos, Koreans, Chinese, and Thai, within the church. Worship services are held separately, in each indigenous language, except on fifth Sundays when all come together for a service of music called "The Sounds of Heaven."

5. Sometimes over a theological shootout, personality conflict, leadership struggle, or disagreement on priorities, a congregation will split. One faction will pull out, start another congregation, and both congregations will prosper more than the one former church did. As Peter Wagner explains, "The people in these churches are like alley cats; they spit and scream, and the net result is more alley cats!"

6. Frequently, an established congregation will strategically plant a daughter congregation, perhaps helping with its initial planning, surveying, staffing, and lay leadership training.

7. The satellite congregation is a newer model in America, having been pioneered in places like Chile and Korea. The Church on the Way (Four Square Gospel) in Van Nuys,

California, has more than two hundred semiautonomous satellite congregations. People hold membership in both the central and satellite congregations. Members meet two Sundays a month in their satellite house-church under a trained leader and the other two Sundays at one of the five worship services of the central congregation.

8. And sometimes a Christian church will arise more or less spontaneously, as in the case of Our Lord's Community Church, in Oklahoma City, Oklahoma, a new congregation of the Reformed Church of America. We close with a case study of this congregation, for it models a reasonable expectation for many new congregations, and it illustrates a number of proven principles in new church planting. Dr. Hunter recently observed this church.

A Concluding Case Study

Our Lord's Community Church of Oklahoma City was constituted in November, 1976, as the first congregation of the Reformed Church of America in that city, as an early expression of the southwest strategy of that denomination's present church growth emphasis. The church's name reflects the denomination's contention that, on balance, denominational labels are not a draw for outsiders, that it is important that the church be perceived as essentially Christian and for the people, with little possibly negative connotations in the name. This strategy was pioneered by celebrated congregations in the Reformed Church, such as Garden Grove Community Church in California and Marble Collegiate Church in New York City. The Reverend Robert Wise, with ten yers of pastoral experience behind him, moved to Oklahoma City to become founding pastor.

A nucleus of just five persons who wanted an R.C.A. congregation in Oklahoma City started this church. They, with Robert Wise, built a membership of 150 members by the day the church was officially constituted. By the summer of 1979 they had over 500 members, with an average worship attendance of 500, and with some 350 persons per week involved in learning experiences. About 200 members are graduates of the Bethel Bible Series.

They launched out with an honest sense of risk and spiritual venturing and with little else by way of resources. Wise explains that "for some time I had wanted to walk out on a limb so far that if God didn't hold it up, I would fall off." He knew that great missionary ventures always begin with trusting God for what will be needed to achieve his purpose. Wise confesses, "I was willing to jeopardize my career in order to validate this conviction." He understandably concludes that "the spiritual attitude of the founding pastor is critical to the new church's success."

More than one-third of the church's five hundred members are new Christians. Another third were inactive, very nominal church people who are now vital Christians for the first time in their lives. The last third were active in churches, but were looking for an alternative congregation. Wise, with a doctorate in the church renewal literatures, has consistently targeted the church's appeal to undiscipled persons and to nominal and inactive Christians in need of renewal ministries and experiences.

Most of the new members have consistently come from within the ever-growing social web of the church's active membership. The members, who have come to love their church and believe it can meet people's needs, feel free to invite their friends, neighbors, relatives, and colleagues. Our Lord's Community Church is a high expectation church. Generally people are not asked to join, they ask to join. All who join take six weeks of orientation and are expected to tithe and to serve as they have gifts for ministry.

The worship service combines serious liturgical structure with spontaneity. The worship service does not feature a choir; the congregation is the choir and does all the responses that a choir would normally do. The worship projects the conscious and clear self-image of the church and its leadership. These Christians want to be a biblical congregation within the general Reformed tradition.

The leaders started their bold experiment with three clear goals: (1) to be lay oriented, not clergy dominated. They want to recognize, affirm, free, and express the people's gifts for ministries; (2) to be a church with an authentic sense of *community;* (3) to be a center of true biblical faith, where people can find *spiritual* answers to their problems, not just answers from sociology or psychology.

The pastor's own conscious priority is "to develop a congregation that can effectively minister to people in need, . . . especially people outside institutional Christianity."

The first meeting place was a YMCA building, which permitted common neutral ground for early interested people. This setting provided a sense of adventure and seemed to create a very quick sense of ownership within many persons. Later a good church facility was purchased, at a reasonable price, from another church who assumed that "a church in this location can't grow any more." The congregation began in their new building by widening their appeal, becoming consciously a metropolitan regional church for the northwest sector of Oklahoma City. In the second year an associate minister was added to the staff and in the third year a clinical psychologist. The rationale for early staff additions is "the ministry of lay development." The leaders wanted to provide training and experiences that would facilitate the people's gifts for ministries. And they wanted a full-service church even though it was new. This staffing and lay involvement has permitted the introduction of exciting new ministries, such as Kingsgate School for sixty handicapped children and a Family Life Center.

Our Lord's Community Church provides an interesting

contrast to the well-known church growth theories of Robert Schuller, also of the Reformed Church in America. First, Our Lord's Community Church is not clergy dominated. Wise discovered that you *motivate* laypeople by including them, giving them legitimate ownership. Wise reports that "at every point we involve as many people as possible, as deeply as possible, in the decision-making process so that they are really shaping their church."

Second, Wise represents the consensus vision of the church's leadership in professing that "our goal is *not* to become One Big Church in this city, but to be a congregation that spawns other congregations." So this church, less than three years old at this writing, already has definite plans for starting another congregation in the next twelve to eighteen months!

May stories like this be recorded, told, and celebrated thousands of times in the next generation. This is one part of a vision that increasingly occupies my mind. The vision includes every nation and every people on earth, but perhaps especially the United States of America. Here about sixty million practicing Christians face 110 million marginal Christians and fifty-five million consciously non-Christian men and women. Let us call this huge block of humanity "the functionally unchurched in America today." It is composed of 165 million people, multitudes of them dissatisfied with their idols and searching for something else, potentially receptive to the Gospel in unprecedented numbers.

I see the mainline denominations and the newer denominations of the United States and the three hundred thousand congregations gearing for growth. Under their loving and vigorous ministry, I see *seventy-five million* (half of the functionally unchurched) becoming responsible, informed Christians, living members of living congregations. Many of these will be in existing congregations. Others will be in new congregations.

119

I hope that both mainline and evangelical denominations will not be content merely to win back the numbers they lost in the past decade. That is a petty goal for churches as large and powerful as most American denominations. Pray for and work toward a great new harvest by the year 2000.

Notes

I. The Discovery of Church Growth

1. Donald McGavran, *Bridges of God* (New York: Friendship Press, 1955).
2. Donald McGavran, *How Churches Grow* (London: World Dominion Press, 1965; New York: Friendship Press, 1955).
3. Donald McGavran, *Understanding Church Growth* (Grand Rapids: Eerdmans Publishing Co., 1970).
4. C. Peter Wagner, *Your Church Can Grow* (Glendale: Regal Books, 1976).
5. C. Peter Wagner, *Your Church Can Be Healthy* (Nashville: Abingdon, 1979).
6. Donald McGavran and Winfield Arn, *How to Grow a Church* (Glendale: Regal Books, 1973).
7. Donald McGavran and Winfield Arn, *Ten Steps to Church Growth* (New York: Harper & Row, 1977).

II. The Key Strategy: Finding the Bridges of God

1. J. Waskom Pickett, *Christian Mass Movements in India* (New York: Abingdon, 1933).
2. *Ibid.*, p. 45.
3. *Ibid.*
4. For more information on receptivity theory in church growth thinking and guidelines for discovering receptive people see McGavran, *Understanding Church Growth*, ch. 12, "The Receptivity of Men and Societies"; and C. Peter Wagner, *Frontiers in Missionary Strategy* (Chicago: Moody Press, 1972), ch. 6, "Anticipatory Strategy." For treatments with an American focus, see McGavran and Arn, *How to Grow a Church*, ch. 3, "Discovering Responsiveness," and George G. Hunter III, *The Contagious Congregation: Frontiers in Evangelism and*

Church Growth (Nashville: Abingdon, 1979), ch. 5, "The Grand Strategy: Discovering Receptive People."

5. See *Church Growth Bulletin*, Vol. XIII, Winter 1977.
6. See Lyle E. Schaller, "Six Targets for Growth," *The Lutheran*, September 3, 1975.
7. See Lyle E. Schaller, "Why Churches Don't Grow," *The Lutheran*, January 19, 1977.
8. Schaller, "Six Targets for Growth."
9. Douglas Hyde, a former Communist converted to Catholicism, delineates in *Dedication and Leadership* (Notre Dame: University of Notre Dame Press, 1966) how Communists require new converts to immediately become involved publicly as practicing Communists—a strategy they borrowed from historic Christianity and which quickly establishes the new convert in his new chosen identity.
10. For an excellent new study of the small church, see Carl S. Dudley, *Making the Small Church Effective* (Nashville: Abingdon, 1978). Dudley delineates the essence of the small church as a single-caring cell.

III. Motivating Local Church People for Church Growth

1. See Abraham H. Maslow, *Motivation and Personality* (New York: Harper & Row, 1970), pp. 23, 55. Maslow emphasizes that "it is unusual, *not* usual, that an act or a conscious wish have but one motivation," p. 23.
2. Lyle E. Schaller, "The Passive Church," *Church Management: The Clergy Journal*, Vol. 54, July 1978.
3. Michael Green, *Evangelism in the Early Church* (Grand Rapids: Eerdmans Publishing Co., 1970), p. 236.
4. *Ibid.*, p. 238.
5. *Ibid.*, p. 253.
6. Probably the best book for our purposes on spiritual gifts for ministry is C. Peter Wagner, *Your Spiritual Gifts Can Help Your Church Grow* (Glendale: Regal Books, 1979).
7. For a summary of the research that backs these contentions, see Wagner, *Frontiers in Missionary Strategy*, ch. 8. For the latest, and most expanded, version of these steps see Wagner, *Your Spiritual Gifts Can Help Your Church Grow*, ch. 4.

IV. Training the Laity for Church Growth

1. Dean M. Kelley, *Why Conservative Churches Are Growing* (New York: Harper & Row, 1972).
2. Virgil Gerber, *God's Way to Keep a Church Going and Growing* (Glendale: Regal Books, 1973).

V. Helping the "Small Church" Grow

1. See Floyd V. Filson's article, "The Significance of the Early House Churches," *The Journal of Biblical Literature*, Vol. LVIII (1939), pp. 105-12.

2. See Lyle E. Schaller, "Looking at the Small Church: A Frame of Reference," *The Christian Ministry,* Vol. VIII, July 1977.
3. This helpful metaphorical approach is from an unpublished resource by L. Ray Sells, *Growth and Evangelism for the Small Church.*
4. Jackson W. Carroll, ed., *Small Churches Are Beautiful* (New York: Harper & Row, 1977).
5. For the description of this situation see Wagner, *Your Church Can Be Healthy,* ch. 3.
6. See chapter 3.
7. Dudley, *Making the Small Church Effective.*
8. For a helpful description of this process see Dudley, *Making the Small Church Effective,* ch. 3.
9. Dudley, p. 52.
10. Lyle E. Schaller in "Looking at the Small Church" also suggests that it is "very, very difficult" for central fellowship groups to divide. The reason for the difficulty is that "the glue which holds this supersaturated group together is far too strong for the members to break in order to divide into smaller groups."
11. See chapter 2.
12. For two complementary but contrasting views of the role of the pastor in church growth, see Lyle E. Schaller and Charles A. Tidwell, *Creative Church Administration* (Nashville: Abingdon, 1975), ch. 7, and Wagner, *Your Church Can Grow,* ch. 4. Other books by Schaller, notably *The Pastor and the People: Building a New Partnership for Effective Ministry* (Nashville: Abingdon, 1973); *Survival Tactics in the Parish* (Nashville: Abingdon, 1977); and *Effective Church Planning* are informative for the church growth pastor.
13. Schaller, "Looking at the Small Church." Italics mine.
14. *Ibid.*
15. See chapter 6.

VI. Reaching People Through New Congregations

1. Lyle E. Schaller, "Why Start New Churches?" *The Circuit Rider,* May 1979, p. 3.
2. See McGavran, *Understanding Church Growth,* ch. 14, "Halting Due to Redemption and Lift."
3. For ways to develop strategy for this near-neighbor or social network evangelism see chapter 2.
4. Schaller, "Why Start New Churches?" p. 5.
5. Ezra E. Jones, *Strategies for New Churches* (New York: Harper & Row, 1976); Carl W. Moorhaus, *Growing New Churches* (Harvey, Ill.: published privately, 1975); F. J. Redford, *Planting New Churches* (Nashville: Broadman Press, 1979).